Member Tips and Problem Solvers

Member Tips and Problem Solvers

Printed in 2005.

Handyman Club of America
12301 Whitewater Drive
Minnetonka, Minnesota 55343
www.handymanclub.com

6 7 8 9 10 / 09 08 07 06 05
© 1995 by Handyman Club of America
ISBN 0-914697-64-1

Printed in the United States of America

CREDITS
Created by The Handyman Club of America Staff
Hal Handy, Contributing Writer
Jeremy Powers, Contributing Editor

Design
Zins Design Studio
Scott Zins, Deb Iacono

Illustrations
RKB Studios, Inc.
Brian Jensen, Mark Begge, Leslie Jensen

Cover Photography courtesy of Cy DeCosse Incorporated.

All brand names used in this book are the property of their owners.

This Handyman Club of America
Member Tips and Problem Solvers is a collection
of helpful information contributed
by
Club Members and the devoted Club staff.
This book is dedicated
to
Handyman Club Members
who provided tips and hints for fellow Members
and to all those who share their skills
and knowledge with others.

Member Tips and Problem Solvers

Complete Handyman's Library™
Handyman Club of America
Minneapolis, Minnesota

Contents

Introduction

The do-it-yourselfer is always looking for easier ways to do things. It's not that the handyman or handywoman is lazy; in fact just the opposite. In most cases, it's only by doing things the best way possible that things work out to be easy on our minds. We don't want to be riddled with some voice of conscience that says, "If only I had done it this way." In other words, what we really want is a satisfying project – to know it's a job well done. If it's easy on our backs, so much the better.

Collected in the Handyman Club of America's *Member Tips and Problem Solvers* are the wisdom and knowledge of more than one hundred Club Members. Some of the Members collected these tips from professionals in the various fields, or from their fathers and sons or from fellow do-it-yourselfers. But most of these simple ideas were created by Members after they put their fertile minds to a problem that perplexed and frustrated them. Many times, these tips are the results of mistakes – they've been paid for in blood, sweat and toil.

In addition to saving some perspiration, *Member Tips and Problem Solvers* is likely to create some inspiration. Several of these tips have been made one better when someone else with a similar experience sees it and adds some extra information or yet another way to do it. You probably will too. We hope that this book will be the first in a series for Handyman Club Members and that our wealth of how-to information continues to grow.

We organized these tips by where you might use them. We figured that there were three basic areas where a handyman plies his trade: outside the home, inside the home and in the shop. Many of the tips belong in more than one area. Tips about caulking for instance, are useful outdoors when painting the house and inside when installing a bath tub. We've tried to classify each tip according to where it would be most useful.

In **Home Exteriors** tips, you'll find hints and ideas on basic construction, exterior painting and staining, roofing, lawn and garden and windows and doors.

In **Home Interiors** tips, there are better ways to do typical jobs of plumbing, electrical, kitchen and bath, heating and cooling, drywall, finish coatings and flooring.

In the **Shop** tips, you'll find suggestions on tools, woodworking and a section on projects.

Some of the tips are more than just tips, so we made them projects. For instance, Member Al Perkins of Show Low, Ariz., sent in a useful way to make your own table saw out of a sheet of plywood. It's a great idea for a way to make the ol' circular saw do double duty, but it takes a little more than few straight cuts and drilling a few holes.

Along with tips, we added a **Reference** section. It includes information regarding grades of plywood, an ownership inspection checklist, project guides, safety precautions and other vital information that's sometimes hard to track down when you need it.

Member Tips and Problem Solvers will help you in projects you're working on and projects you haven't dreamed of. These tips will save you money, reduce frustration, make your projects look better and inspire to do even more. In addition, *Member Tips and Problem Solvers* will provide some fun, inspirational reading between projects that will make you say, "Gee! I should have thought of that!"

HOME EXTERIORS

- Construction
- Paint/Stain/Clean
- Roofing
- Windows and Doors

Construction

Remove Small Trees–Stump and All

Trees up to 8 inches in diameter can be removed, stump and all, by using the trunk as a lever. Trim off the branches and dig around the base of the tree, cutting roots as they are encountered. Meanwhile, pull on the tree with a rope that is tied as high as possible up the trunk to gain leverage. Continue until all roots are cut and the tree is felled.

Charles Parker
Aurora, Colorado

How to Cut Rigid Foam Insulation

When cutting sheets of rigid foam insulation, it's much easier if you first lean the sheet against a wall. Then insert utility knives at each end of the line to cut, lay your straight-edge on the knives and cut along it. This is much easier than marking a line and trying to follow it.

Brett Siepert
Rexburg, Idaho

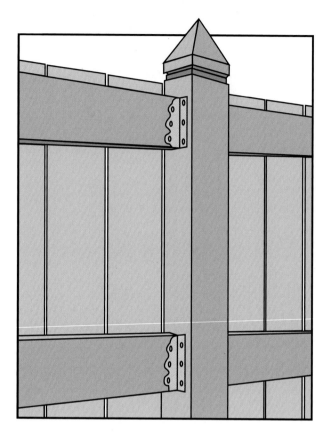

Handy Board Fence Construction

In the construction of "board fences," hang sections of fencing between the upright posts by using 2"x4" joist hangers on the posts. This makes it easy to repair fence sections or posts and simplifies moving sections of fence. If you attach the hangers with screws it means you don't have to pound on newly set posts, either.

Charles Parker
Aurora, Colorado

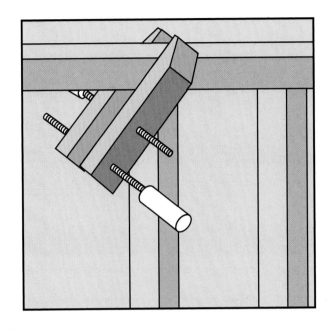

Keep Concrete and Grout Mix Dry

Don't let leftover mortar or concrete mix soak up moisture and harden in the bag. Use a clean, dry funnel and pour it into gallon milk jugs and cap the containers. The top half of 2-liter soda bottles make great funnels. This doesn't waste the material and keeps it handy for small repairs.

Harold Van Arsdale
Ponca City, Oklahoma

Clamp Down on Warped Lumber

A "C" clamp or wooden screw clamp is helpful for bringing adjoining framing members into alignment. The large jaws of a 12-inch clamp make it easy to twist studs, trimmers, plates and other warped lumber into the same plane for nailing or screwing.

Hal Handy

Remove Roots Near Underground Pipes or Wires

To cut away tree roots in an area where the use of an ax is impractical, such as near underground pipes or wiring, use a large wood chisel and mallet. For smaller roots, a tree limb lopper–the one with long handles and a small jaw–works well, too.

Charles Parker
Aurora, Colorado

Build Friendly Forms for Concrete Steps

When building forms for concrete steps, the bottom of the riser (vertical) boards should be beveled at about a 45-degree angle. This allows the edge of finishing trowel to reach under the board so the tread can be finished without removing the forms.

Hal Handy

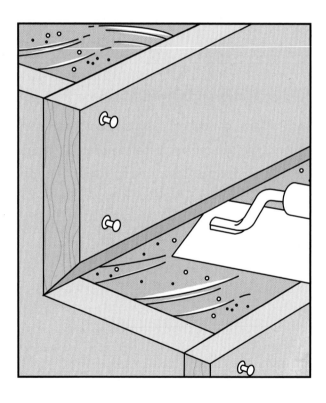

How Much Concrete?

The following table will help determine how many cubic feet or cubic yards of mixed concrete you'll need for a slab. To use it, figure the total area to be covered in square feet. Then, look under the column for the desired thickness of the slab you want. The cubic feet chart is best if you're mixing your own concrete because that's the way bags of concrete mix come. The cubic yard chart is best if you're ordering ready-mixed concrete because that's the way the ready mix provider will want it. For sizes or quantities not listed here, add or multiply figures. For example, for a 5-inch slab, add the quantities for a 2-inch and a 3-inch slab. For a 60 sq. ft. slab, multiply the amount needed for a 20-foot slab of the same thickness by 3.

Quantity of Concrete for Slab Thickness

Sq. ft.		2"	3"	4"	6"
15	cu. ft.	2.5	3.75	5.0	7.5
	cu. yd.	0.1	0.15	0.2	0.3
20	cu. ft.	3.3	5.0	6.7	10.0
	cu. yd.	0.1	0.2	0.3	0.4
50	cu. ft.	8.3	12.51	6.7	25.0
	cu. yd.	0.3	0.5	0.6	0.9
75	cu. ft.	12.5	18.75	25.0	37.5
	cu. yd.	0.5	0.7	0.9	1.4
100	cu. ft.	16.7	25.0	33.3	50.0
	cu. yd.	0.6	0.9	1.2	1.9
150	cu. ft.	25.0	37.5	50.0	75.0
	cu. yd.	0.9	1.4	1.9	2.8
200	cu. ft.	33.3	50.0	66.7	100.0
	cu. yd.	1.2	1.9	2.5	3.7

Protect Buried Underground Cable

When burying any kind of cable in your yard (television or phone), run them through lengths of inexpensive PVC pipe to protect them from the elements, rodents or from being cut by shovels.

Charles Parker
Aurora, Colorado

Lawn and Garden

Peat Moss Mulch Helps Start Seeded Lawns

Several seed and fertilizer companies have new seed and mulch mixes on the market designed to re-seed bare areas of a lawn. The mixture is grass seed, a mild fertilizer and ground-up newspaper for mulch. It's much cheaper to buy bulk grass seed and mulch it with Canadian sphagnum peat moss. First rake the area to soften the soil. Then spread the area thick with grass seeds. Apply one inch of peat moss and spread it around with an upside down leaf rake. Then water it well and water it daily. Within weeks the grass will grow and you won't be able to see much of the leftover peat moss.

Jeremy Powers
Fridley, Minnesota

Dish Soap Bottles Get Oil in Tight Spots

Getting motor oil into a lawnmower, tiller or other outdoor power equipment can be messy. Funnels sometimes help, but many times there isn't room near the oil port to stand a funnel upright. And, it's easy to overfill a funnel. Instead, clean out a liquid dishwashing bottle that has a push-pull dispenser cap and fill it with oil. The spout can be positioned directly over the oil filler port before opening and then quickly shut when the reservoir is full. These bottles also work great for garden tools like the blades of hedge trimmers and for chain saw bar oil, either put it on the chain saw or add a little to the bar where you need it most.

Roger Brinson
Ashland, Virginia

Choose Local Stone for Landscaping

If you want to save time and money with your landscaping projects, choose a local stone. Whether it is river rock, pea gravel, lava rock or some other crushed stone, you can probably buy plenty of it from a local supplier without paying for packaging or shipping. For instance, in the Midwest, lava rock is expensive because it comes from the Pacific Northwest. It costs about $4 a cubic foot at the garden center. Local river rock costs $4 a cubic yard.

Jeremy Powers
Fridley, Minnesota

Put Your Downspouts to Work in the Garden

One of the best ways to divert rainwater away from your foundation is to channel the water from your downspouts to rock gardens, via underground drain tile. Because of the force of the moving water, use stone rather than mulch around plants to prevent water erosion.

Don Hedquist
Minneapolis, Minnesota

Prevent Battery Cable Corrosion

One of the problems with many self-starting lawn mowers and garden tractors is corrosion around battery terminals. This corrosion is a result of oxidation and makes for hard starting and damages battery cables and terminals. This corrosion may be prevented by buying chemical treated disks to place on the terminals, but a simple way is to apply petroleum jelly, such as Vaseline,™ over the terminal. This seals the various metal parts, such as the copper cable, steel cable terminal and the lead battery terminal, from the air and moisture.

Clayton L. Hewes
Canton, New York

Mulch Fights Weeds Better than Stone

If you're putting down rock to combat weeds in a landscaping project, use mulch from your lawn instead. Several inches of decomposing grass and leaves will give off an acid that will reduce weed growth there. Some weeds will grow through as much as six inches of rock, even with a plastic barrier.

Willie Vogt
Eagan, Minnesota

Clamp on Wood to Loosen Lawnmower Blades

To remove a lawnmower blade quickly and easily, use a C-clamp to clamp a small block of wood to the inside of the lawnmower housing so that the wood is in the path of the blade. The same block can be used to tighten it when reinstalling.

Jeremy Powers
Fridley, Minnesota

Painless Post Pulling

Here's a nearly sweat-free way to remove deep-set posts. It's called a lever. Stand a 10-ft-long, 4"x4" timber alongside the post you want to remove and loosely wrap a heavy chain around the post and timber about 6 inches from the ground. Then swing the 4"x4" down over an old automobile wheel and push down on the free end. The closer you place the wheel to the post, the greater the mechanical advantage created by the lever-and-fulcrum action and the easier it is.

Gene Jordon
Farmington, Connecticut

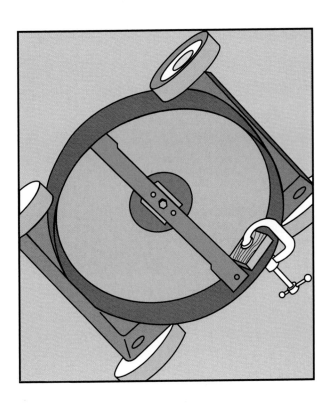

17

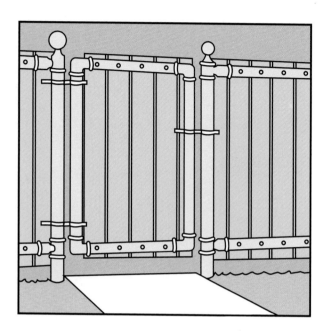

Paint/Stain/ Clean

How to Make Lightweight Gates

To provide a lightweight frame for a gate in a large wooden fence, make a top rail from chain link pipe and use chain link fittings to hang gate parts.

Charles Parker
Aurora, Colorado

Grass Won't Stick to WD-40

Before each use of your lawnmower, spray the underside with WD-40. Then even wet grass clippings won't stick to the underside. It makes clean up much easier. This is particularly important when you have one of the newer mulching mowers where the underside of the mower serves as a vital part of the mulching process rather than just protecting people from the moving blade.

Sidney H. Hersh
Silver Springs, Maryland

Solvent-Free Brush Clean Up

There is an alternative to using solvent to clean oil-based paint from brushes. Wipe off the excess paint with a rag. Then put a little hand cleaner, like GoJo or Goop, on the bristles. Work it through for about a minute and rinse the brush under warm water. Don't try this with natural bristle brushes. Water causes natural bristles to swell.

Leo Wagman
Carlton, Minnesota

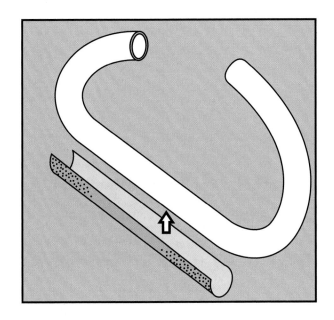

Sanding Flutes a Pipe Dream

Sanding fluted porch columns and trim boards on a Victorian house can be a difficult job. A heat gun can remove most paint, but the flutes still need to be sanded before repainting. Take a piece of PVC water pipe, and with a heat gun, bend it into a "D" shape. The straight part is for sanding and the curved portion becomes a handle. Use contact cement to fasten coarse sandpaper around this useful tool.

Hal Handy

Homemade Paint Strainer

Never discard used nylon stockings or panty hose. They make great paint strainers. Cut the legs of the nylons into 12-inch lengths, tie a knot in one end and you have homemade, inexpensive strainers.

Gerald Hawkins
Rupert, Idaho

Rim Holes Prevent Paint Splashes

When opening a new can of paint, drive 6 to 8 holes in the inside lip of the can so paint can run back into the can. This lip, which holds the lid on, catches paint naturally and if allowed to fill, creates a mess when you close the can. Punch the holes with a small finishing or box nail. Don't use a drill, because little bits of metal from the can will cause rust stains on your wall.

David W. Ziemek
Arlington Heights, Illinois

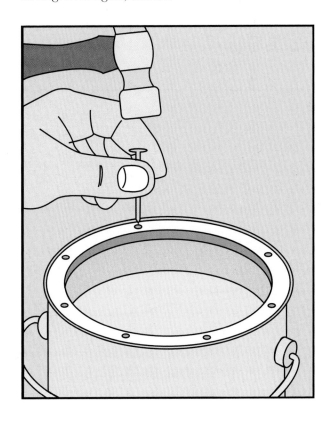

19

Prevent Paint Seepage Under Masking Tape

When masking off baseboards or other trim in preparation for painting a wall, there is a way to get near-perfect results. First, wash the trim with mild detergent and dry. Use only new, soft masking tape. Then use one continuous piece of masking tape from corner to corner. After the tape is placed on the lip of the base, take a stiff putty knife and slide it firmly on top of the tape to secure it. This will prevent any paint seepage and reduce the need for cleanup.

Greg Stultz
Chicago, Illinois

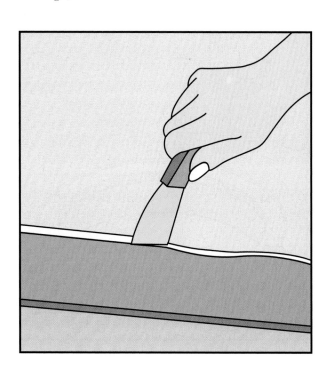

Prevent Spills from Running Down Your Arms

Most handymen know that when painting or cleaning something over their heads, they wear protective gloves and glasses for safety against paint and harsh chemicals. Go one step further to prevent liquids from running down your arms. Fold out cuffs on the gloves to catch any extra liquid from running down your arm. Periodically you'll need to clean out the "gutters."

Lina Grigaitis
Northbrook, Illinois

Keep Paint Supply Clean

When you paint or varnish, pour small amounts for use into a separate can or container. This way, the unused paint in the can is not contaminated and will be ready to go for your next project. Any left-over paint should be strained back into the original can using old nylons or pantyhose.

Greg Stultz
Chicago, Illinois

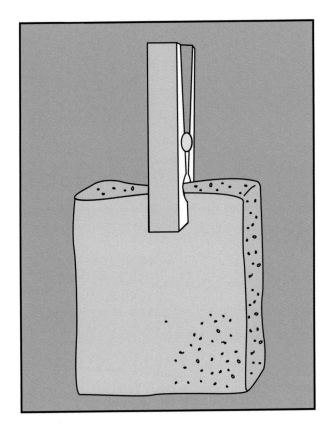

Make Your Own Throw Away Foam Brushes

If you like to keep a good supply of cheap, disposable brushes on hand for small touch-up jobs, try making your own. Save foam blocks used as packaging material or buy small slabs at a craft store. Cut the foam on a band saw to the desired thickness, length and width. For handles, use snap-type clothes pins. For added strength, a piece from a plastic lid can be cut to the same shape as the foam and clamped with the clothes pin against one side. No clean-up is necessary. Just throw away the foam and reuse the handle.

Jerry L. Vess
Mt. Eaton, Ohio

A New Way to Look at Storing Paint

Store your paint cans upside down. The paint forms a tight seal around the inverted lid so air can't get inside and cause a skin to form. Clean the rim where the lid seats to ensure a good seal and make sure the lids are on tight before you flip the cans.

John Dennis
Lake Havasu City, Arizona

Neater Paint Job with a Brush Wiper

Wiping a paint brush on the lip of a paint can always leaves paint in the groove of the can. Soon, the paint is dripping down the outside of the can. Try stretching a piece of strapping tape or duct tape across the top of the opened can and pinch the sticky sides together. It makes a handy, and effective, brush-wiping edge.

Handyman Club Staff

How much paint?

The following chart will help you determine how much paint you'll need for the job you're doing. The amounts in the first column are for a first coat. The amounts in the second column are for a second coat. A second coat usually only requires about two-thirds as much paint as a first coat.

Paint Coverage Per Gallon

Surface to cover	First Coat	Second Coat
Exterior rough or porous surface	90-110 sq. ft.	135-160 sq. ft.
Exterior smooth surface	375-425 sq. ft.	560-600 sq. ft.
Interior rough or porous surface	120-190 sq. ft.	180-275 sq. ft.
Interior smooth surface	420-490 sq. ft.	600-700 sq. ft.

Roofing

Asphalt

A Painter's Brick Trick

When painting around brick, keep a small piece of the same brick (or one that's similar in color) handy. If you drip on the brick, immediately blot it up with a rag. Then rub the spot with the loose piece of brick. The dust created will be absorbed, coloring the paint spot to match the brick.

Arthur Elson
Troy, Ohio

Make Your Drip Edge Drip

The metal "D" drip edge commonly used on the bottom edge of a shingled roof should be rebent to the proper angle so that it lays in the same plane as the roof. If installed as bent in the factory, the edge often raises the roof edge so water ponds behind the edge and can leak under shingles or dribble down the fascia board.

Hal Handy

Rain Gutters in the Ground

An alternative to gutters for roof water disposal is a shallow trench in the ground under the drip line of the eaves. Dig the trench 10 inches deep and taper the cut back toward the foundation. Line the trench with black polyethylene, and lay a perforated drain tile in the bottom of the trench. Cover the tile and fill the trench with washed gravel. The tile can be drained to a low corner of the lot or to a storm sewer or curb. As the water drips from the roof edge, it will fall into the gravel bed. The plastic will direct it away from the foundation and into the perforated tile. If the gravel becomes covered with leaves, the water will still find its way into the gravel and be drained away. Flowers or shrubs can be grown in pots or tubs set into the gravel. Washed gravel or marble chips should be used, not crushed limestone. Limestone will dissolve over time.

Hal Handy

Seal Shingle Side Tabs, Too

Modern self-sealing shingles seal the bottom edge of the tab to the shingle below. But shingle tabs at an exposed edge, like at the edge of the roof, should be completely sealed down with roofing cement, too. This prevents wind, rain and snow from getting under the shingles at these points. This is particularly important for the last shingle on the ridge row. Ridge shingles should always be lapped away from the prevailing wind.

Hal Handy

Reset a Protruding Roofing Nail

If a roofing nail or staple works its way up and raises an asphalt shingle tab, the nail or staple can be reset without making a hole in the tab. It requires two wide-blade putty or drywall knives. Insert one knife under the raised shingle tab and over the backed-out nail or staple. The second is placed over the shingle tab above the first. A hammer can then be used to drive the nail or staple back into the sheathing without damaging the shingle.

Hal Handy

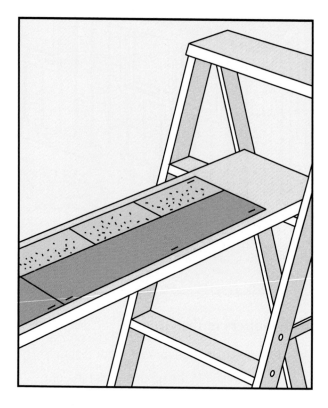

Walk Safely on Leftover Shingles

Leftover asphalt shingles can be tacked to scaffolding, planks, and other walking surfaces to provide better traction during wet, frosty, or muddy weather. They provide better grip than wooden cleats and are not affected by rain. Even if you have to buy a bundle of shingles for this purpose, they are cheap protection against nasty falls.

Hal Handy

Wood

Hike Up Those Shingles

If you don't feel safe carrying an 80-pound bundle of asphalt shingles up a ladder to the roof, and splitting the bundles makes them too flexible and hard to handle, here's a slick trick. Build a compact plywood box, open at the top and sized to hold the shingles. Now, both hands will be free while climbing with the weight properly supported on your back and hips to reduce the chance of injury.

Hal Handy

How to Apply New Wood Shingles

When applying new wood shingles, either sawn or split, the butts of the shingles should be sealed with oil-based paint. Either dip the shingles in a shallow pan of paint or paint the butts with a brush while they're still strapped in the bundle. The paint will seal the end grain of the shingles so that water will not be absorbed by capillary attraction. Water absorption at the butt end is the most common cause of failure for wood shingles.

Hal Handy

25

How to Make Replaced Wood Shingles Match

When replacing damaged cedar shingles or shakes, the obvious color difference between new and old shingles can be minimized. Soak the new shingles in a solution of one pound of baking soda in a gallon of water. Exposure to the sun will cause a photochemical reaction in the cedar that will permanently gray the shingle in 4 to 6 hours.

Hal Handy

Extend the Life of a Wood Roof

If the slope and height of the roof permit, the life of a wood shingle roof can be extended by sweeping the roof at least once a year. All the debris, which accumulates in the cracks between the shingles, should be swept out. Cleaning the valleys is particularly important. A power washer can be used, but it may make the roof too slippery for safe working.

Hal Handy

Mildew and Moss Growth on Shingles

Mildew and moss growth on shingles, either wood or asphalt, can be minimized. Insert a strip of copper or zinc under the bottom edge of the top row of shingles and leave about an inch exposed. Rain will cause a very diluted solution of copper or zinc sulfate to wash down the roof. This solution will kill the moss and inhibit mildew growth. For a large roof, a second strip halfway down the roof may be needed.

If the moss problem is severe, as in a heavily shaded site, the moss can be killed by spraying the roof with 2,4-D (common broadleaf weed killer) or a solution of copper sulfate (usually sold as Bordeaux Mixture). The moss can be removed with a high-pressure washer if you use it carefully to avoid damaging the shingles. If the shingles are wood, be careful working on the roof. Wood shingles, sawn or split, are extremely slippery when wet.

Hal Handy

Windows and Doors

How to Reputty Windows

Reputtying windows can get a bit frustrating, even for a pro. The trick is good putty consistency. The consistency of glazing compound (window putty) varies by manufacturer, age of the compound and even from the top to the bottom of the same can. The best way to change the consistency of glazing compound is to knead in a few drops of Penetrol, an oil-based paint additive. It seems to make the glazing compound more plastic and adhesive than other paint thinners. It takes just a few drops for a sizable ball of material.

Hal Handy

Secure Sliding Glass Doors

A sliding glass door can be made more secure by adding a thin block of wood in the top track at the latch side of the door. The block should be just a few inches long and thick enough to just clear the top of the door when it shuts. This block prevents a burglar from using a pry bar to raise the door off the track and then kicking in the door. When the door is opened past the block, it can still be lifted off the track for repairs and cleaning. A large-headed screw, screwed up into the header, can be used in the same way, and may be less visible than the block of wood.

Hal Handy

Aluminum Combination Windows

Aluminum combination storm windows should never be caulked or sealed at the bottom. In the summer, when the storm panel is raised and the screen is in place, wind-blown rain can push a considerable amount of water through the screen. Many combination units have drain holes along the bottom rail. Others depend on a rather loose fit to let this water out. If it cannot drain, it will soak into the sill, causing rot. This trapped water may run down inside the wall to cause paint peeling and other problems, too. If there are no drainage holes, two or three ⅛-inch holes can be drilled through the storm window frame at the sill.

Hal Handy

Preserve a Used Tube of Caulk for Reuse

Preserving a partially used tube of caulk has challenged nearly every do-it-yourselfer. One good solution is to leave an inch or two of caulk extending from the nozzle. When it hardens it becomes a handle to pull out the hardened caulk in the tip. A variation on this is to use a short length of the plastic jacket from electrical cable. Press the jacket over the nozzle and partially fill it with caulk. The caulk sets in the cable jacket, which can be pulled off to expose fresh caulk. (Cable jacket can also be used as an extension nozzle to get caulk into otherwise difficult spots.)

Hal Handy

Protect Those Squeaky Hinges

When faced with a squeaky hinge, a drop or two of Armor-All brand protectant will cure the problem longer than light oil and without any dirty streaks or marks. Because it contains silicone, Armor-All makes a good lubricant for light duty tasks.

Hal Handy

How to Reglaze Wood Windows

When reglazing a wood window, be sure to seal the area that will be covered by new glazing compound. After all of the old putty (glazing compound) is scraped out, seal the newly exposed wood in the glazing channel with oil-based primer or boiled linseed oil. The wood in an old window is so dry that it will absorb the oil from the new glazing compound quickly, leaving it hard, brittle and less effective.

When painting the reglazed window, the paint should cover the glazing compound and about ¹⁄₁₆ of an inch onto the glass. The paint will help seal the joint between the glazing compound and the glass. If you get an excess of paint on the glass, always scrape the paint parallel to the putty, never toward it. The blade should not break the bond between the paint and the glazing compound.

Hal Handy

Condensation on Windows Means Excess Moisture

If there is condensation on the living area side of a window that is double-glazed or is equipped with a storm window, the humidity in the house is too high. Moisture may be condensing inside the walls or in the attic, too, reducing the effectiveness of the insulation there. There are many possible sources of excessive moisture, including: power humidifiers that are set too high, a furnace or water heater which is not venting properly, a damp basement, a crawl space that does not have a plastic ground cover, large numbers of house plants, or aquariums without covers. Moisture moves readily throughout the house, so any ventilation system (venting range hood, bathroom vent fan) will reduce the humidity below the condensation point.

Hal Handy

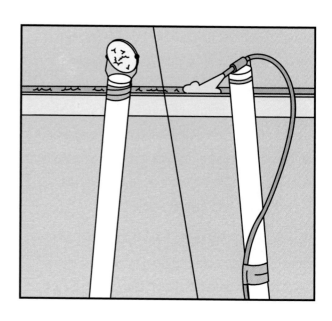

Home Exterior Miscellaneous

Inspect Rain Gutters

To examine the inside of gutters on a two-story house, mount a mirror on a piece of dowel or PVC pipe of an appropriate length so you can view the gutters from the ground. This eliminates cumbersome ladder work. By attaching a garden hose to the same pole, any debris can easily and safely be washed away.

Charles Parker
Aurora, Colorado

Cotter Pin Tool Helps Repair Screens

Removing the old rotted rubber spline when replacing the screen fabric in patio doors and windows can be trouble. Next time try a cotter pin extractor. They work great. These pointed, S-shaped tools also allows you to clean the channel before placing the splines.

John J. Williams
Paulsboro, New Jersey

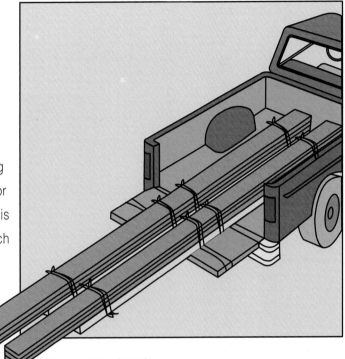

You Can Do It Too

A piece of plywood laid across the top of a strong galvanized trash can makes a convenient table for tools when working on outdoor projects. The can is easily moved, and laying a board across it is much quicker than clamping a shelf onto a sawhorse.

Mark Sande
St. Louis Park, Minnesota

Restore Threads in Plastic Parts

If the threads in a plastic part become stripped, try this method of repair. Fill the female threads with a two-part epoxy glue. Then cut new threads with a tap after the material has set. It helps to rotate the part while the epoxy is hardening. That prevents the glue from sagging and keeps it evenly distributed.

Harold Kelly
Ailen, South Carolina

Long Haul Siding

To carry strips of 16-foot siding on a pickup truck use 14-foot lengths of 2x6s or 2x8s for support. Lash the siding to the lumber and lay it in the bed of the truck.

Charles Parker
Aurora, Colorado

HOME INTERIORS

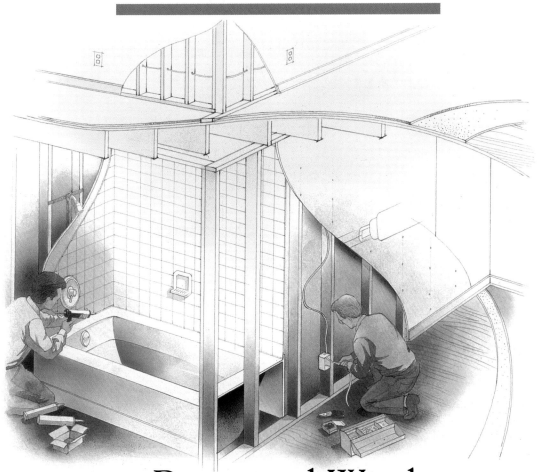

- Doors and Windows
- Flooring
- Mechanical
- Walls

Doors and Windows

Repair Old Doorways

In old houses, sometimes door openings become parallelograms rather than rectangles. Planing the long edge of an old solid door on the door knob side until it no longer interferes with the jamb is the common fix. But it's not the best one because if the overlap of the door onto the jamb is large, the lock and strike may have to be reset. Not only is resetting the knob and latch difficult, it can affect the way the door looks. Instead, the amount of overlap, plus 1/16-inch, should be marked on the hinge side of the door. The door and the hinge are removed and the edge of the door is planed to the mark. The hinge is then remortised and remounted using the same screw holes. The repair will be less obvious and the lock and strike should still match.

Hal Handy

Deal the Cards to Adjust Binding Doors

Over time, some doors begin to bind when the door frame goes slightly out of square. The door can be made to open smoothly again by shimming either the hinge at the top or bottom. A plastic-coated playing card makes a great shim. They're very difficult to compress and you can use one or more to create the thickness for an exact fit.

Hal Handy

Keep Dusty Drafts Out

Contain dust clouds during home remodeling projects by applying heat-shrink window wrap, designed to reduce drafts, over the doorways. Unlike the plastic and tape method of sealing doors, the shrink wrap won't peel paint off the walls when it's removed.

Kevin Sigsby
Salt Lake City, Utah

Support Bi-fold Doors
Pivot Keeps Doors On Track

Bi-fold doors are common doors for closets in modern homes. But just as common are problems of them falling out of their tracks. The main pivot for a bi-fold door is attached to the jamb and rests on the floor. However, if the floor is carpeted, there is nothing solid to support the outer end of the pivot. The jamb attachment is usually inadequate to keep the pivot from sagging. It's the sagging of this pivot that causes most bi-fold doors to fall out of their tracks. The easiest way to support the pivot is to run a drywall screw through the carpet into the flooring so the head supports the end of the pivot. Adjust the correct support height by turning the screw in or out. Whenever screwing through carpet, work slowly in case a burr on the screw grabs a carpet fiber. If the screw catches a fiber while being power driven, the fiber winds around the screw and puts a run in the carpet. Use an awl or a gimlet to start the hole, not a power drill, for the same reason.

Hal Handy

Snug Up Door Hinge Screws

Once a door hinge has been removed, the screws may not tighten up when you reattach it. The best solution is new, longer screws. But sometimes large screws were used in the first place. In those cases, inserting a plastic wall anchor into the hole should help to snug the screws. You can also insert several toothpicks or slivers from cedar shingles, dipped in wood glue, into the hole. Break them off at the surface and let it all dry before inserting the screws.

Rudy D. Harter
Newton, Iowa

Vinyl Molding Makes Good Hinge Shim

To fix a door that has an irregular gap between the strike side of the door and the jamb, use vinyl base molding as a hinge shim. Cut the vinyl molding to fit and slip it between the hinge and hinge jamb. The vinyl doesn't crack or shrink over time. To fix a door that gaps near the floor, place the shim behind the bottom hinge. To correct a door that gaps near the top, place the shim behind the upper hinge. Once the door is properly spaced, re-install the screws.

Stephen Cantelli
Minneapolis, Minnesota

Flooring

Foam Filled Squeaks

When wood stairs or floors in a home develop annoying squeaks, screws and nails aren't the only answer. Instead, inject the problem area with expanding foam. For instance, if a floor joist sags and pulls away from the subflooring above it (a common cause of squeaks), squirt the foam into the gap.

Tom Goffron
Lombard, Illinois

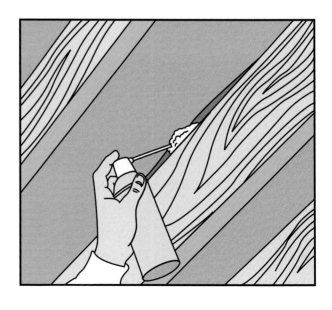

Cut Casings, Not Around Them

Cutting around all the nooks and corners of a typical door casing and jamb can be the worst part of putting in a new floor. Rather than making a complicated cut in ceramic tile, vinyl flooring or hardwood, it's easier to trim the bottom of the door casing so the new flooring can slide under the casing. If you're careful, you don't have to remove the casings to do this. Lay a tile or piece of flooring on the underlayment (upside down to prevent scratching) and use a fine-toothed, small hand saw to cut off the bottom of the casing. Be careful not to cut into the wall or the door jamb. Those flexible Japanese saws, that cut on the pull instead of the push, work great for this.

Hal Handy

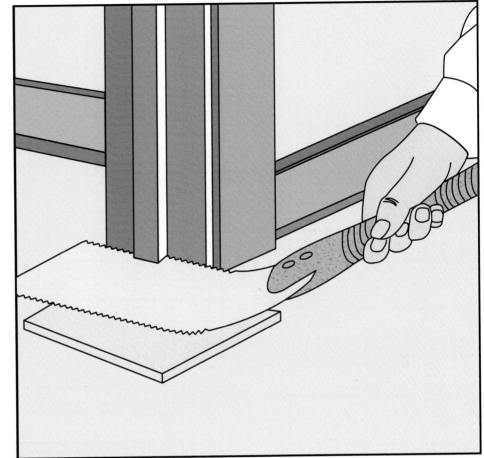

Trowel Slickum' Won't Stickum', Says Wickum

Before applying carpet glue or other flooring adhesives, lightly coat your trowel or putty knife with WD-40. The lubricant won't contaminate the adhesive, but it will prevent it from bonding to your tools, making cleanup a whole lot easier.

Doug Wickum
Peck, Idaho

Mechanical

Electrical

Storing Light Bulbs

To store a typical household's supply of light bulbs, salvage a piece of expanded foam packaging that measures about 13"x13" and is two inches thick. Drill 16 holes in it with a 1¼" hole saw and make them 1½" deep and 3¼" on center. Each hole will hold a bulb so that you can read the wattage and the whole "tray" of bulbs can be carried safely around the house. Even if they're jostled, they won't break.

Robert Guyre
Maywood, New Jersey

A Fixed Electrical "Repair Boxes"

A "repair box" is commonly used to hold new electrical outlets or switches. When working in old houses, the presence of plaster pushed through old wood-lath plaster walls, called plaster keys, sometimes keeps them from seating solidly. If they don't seem to hold in those situations, the boxes can be fastened firmly with a can of do-it-yourself expanding urethane foam. By using the extension tube on the can of foam, inject the foam around the box. When the foam hardens, the box will be held tightly. The foam should never be used inside the box. A certain amount of air is necessary in the box for heat dissipation from the electrical device.

Hal Handy

Stripping Stranded Wire Made Easy

When using stranded wire, trying to wrap it around screws or other items without the strands coming loose can be very frustrating. When stripping stranded wire there is a way to solve this problem. Leave a small piece of insulation at the end to hold the strands in place so they won't come loose when you're working.

Melissa Slattery
Uxbridge, Massachusetts

Heat Strip Wire

When wire strippers are unavailable, simply heat the end of the wire with matches or a lighter. Then wait just a moment, lick your thumb and finger to prevent burning them, and then pinch the softened insulating coating while pulling it off. The wire is unaffected by the heat.

Michael Griffin
Munster, Indiana

Broken Light Bulb? Cork It!

Removing the base of a broken light bulb when the base is stuck in the socket is one of those everyday hazards. You can use a pair of long nose pliers, but even when you know the power is off, working with electricity and steel tools can be unnerving. A better tool is a wine cork from a 1.5 liter bottle of wine (not the type you use a cork screw with, but the type you remove by hand). Simply insert the cork in the broken bulb base and back it out. Again, always turn off the power when working with electricity.

James J. Myers
West Los Angeles, California

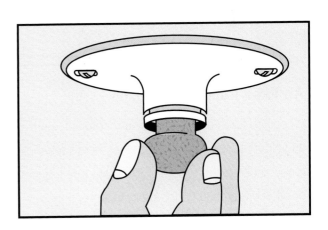

Chains Fish Vertical Wires Better

When you need to fish a wire from one floor to the next, use a chain. It falls straight, not like an electrician's fish tape or line, and the chain falls off obstacles that obstruct part of its path, such as switch boxes and joists.

Jim Ryan
Columbus, Ohio

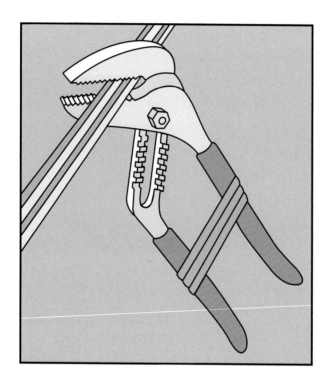

An Extra Rubber Band Hand

When you need a "third hand" on a project, such as soldering several wires together, here's a handy tool you can make yourself. When you buy broccoli or other vegetables at the grocery store, they usually come wrapped with thick, strong rubber bands. Wrap one of those husky rubber bands around the handle of a pair of pliers. It keeps the jaws of the pliers clamped on your work and leaves your hands free.

David Zirnek
Arlington Heights, Illinois

In–The–Wall Angling

Here's an easy way to fish wires through plaster and lath walls. Rather than snag an expensive fish tape on a protruding plaster key, tie an egg sinker from your tackle box to the end of a waxed line and drop it down within the wall. Retrieve the sinker at the bottom, tie the electrical cable to the line and pull it up and out the top hole.

Courtney W. Patton
Liberty Center, Ohio

Use a Cloth to Change Halogen Bulbs

Always use a lint-free cloth when handling halogen light bulbs. The oil from your fingers, can cause the bulb to heat up and burn out in just a few hours. If you accidentally touch the glass, clean it immediately with isopropyl alcohol and a lint-free cloth.

Tremaine Pryor
Nashville, Arkansas

Heating and Cooling Systems

Hack Saws Help Pulling Wires

Pulling wires through electrical conduit can be difficult, especially when the conduit has multiple bends and junction boxes. Here's a solution. Hook and tape an old hacksaw blade to the end of your fish tape after you've run it through the conduit. Then attach the wires to the other end of the blade. The blade doesn't hang up in the conduit and pulls the wires through without snagging.

Arthur Regensburger
Stratford, Connecticut

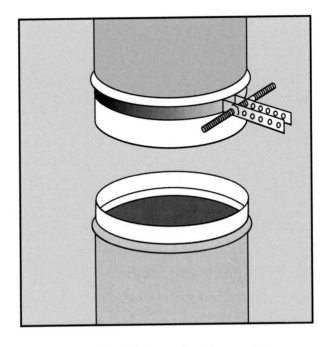

Peel Electrical Cable Like a Potato

Here's a trick for stripping the non-metallic sheathing from interior-type electrical cable (NM-B), the kind most people use in wiring projects in their home or garage. It originally came from an electrician more than a decade ago. Hook the blade of a potato peeler under the flat side of the cable and peel back the outer sheath without fear of nicking the insulation on the wires below.

Stan Willbanks
Apple Valley, Minnesota

Disconnect Prefabricated Chimney Pipe

The interlocking pieces of a prefabricated fireplace chimney lock together well–too well if you want to take them apart again. A length of plumber's strap (flexible perforated metal strapping), a long ¼-inch stove bolt, and two washers can make the equivalent of an oversized hose clamp to compress the upper section enough to uncouple the sections. The plumbers strap is cut to about the circumference of the pipe and bent at right angles at each end. The bolt, with a washer under both the head and nut, is inserted through the holes in the strap ends. Tightening the nut puts the squeeze on the pipe and allows the pieces to snap apart.

Hal Handy

Easy-Out Furnace Filter

Because of close tolerances, it's often necessary to pry a filter from a furnace using a knife or screwdriver. Here's a better idea. Fit the permanent electrostatic filters on a furnace with a pull tab made from duct tape. Then you won't have to worry about damaging the filter's aluminum frame when you remove the element for cleaning.

Don Moseley
Pacific Grove, California

Balance Your Heating and Cooling Systems

An important part of good performance of any comfort conditioning system is balancing the system so the distribution of heated or cooled air is proportional to the loss or gain of each room. Because adjustments are partially based on your perception of comfort it is best done by the home-owner. It will probably take more than one day, but with virtually no work at any one time. Follow this process for the heating season:

Step 1 Open all dampers, including those that may be in the duct system, rather than on the walls. You sometimes have to really look to find the location of all dampers. There may not be any, but there usually are.

Step 2 Adjust the room thermostat to a comfortable temperature.

Step 3 Leave six or more thermometers at table height in various rooms. They need not be expensive or accurate, as long as they all read the same when they are in the same location. Observe them once or twice a day during typical winter weather.

Step 4 Partially close the dampers, preferably in the duct system first, that supply the rooms that are too warm. Usually these will be small rooms or rooms near the furnace. If there are some rooms that still do not get warm enough, partially close the dampers to all the other rooms until the cool rooms reach the desired temperature.

Step 5 When the system is balanced to the temperatures you like (not necessarily all rooms at the same temperature), the damper settings should be marked.

The procedure will need to be repeated during the cooling season, with the dampers being

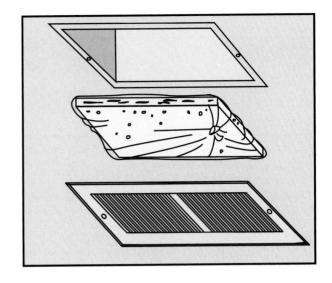

Home Interiors pg 43

partially closed to rooms that overcool until the warmest room reaches a cool enough temperature. The damper settings will be considerably different–almost opposite–than during the heating season. When the desired distribution is reached, mark the summer setting.

After the correct winter and summer settings are marked, the dampers can be reset easily as the seasons change.

If there are rooms that cannot be heated or cooled satisfactorily, it may be necessary to add another duct, wall outlet or booster, but that should be rare in a reasonably well designed system.

Hal Handy

Winterize Your AC Ceiling Vents

If you have an air conditioning system completely separate from the heating system, the outlet diffusers are probably located in the ceiling. In cold climates, it is essential that these diffusers be closed and sealed tightly during the winter. Otherwise, the heated moist air from the rooms will rise into the cooling system duct work, which is located in the attic. The attic will be cool, and the moisture in the inside air will condense, pool in the ducts, and drip out the joints in the ductwork. This can ruin the ducts, surrounding insulation and even the ceiling. If not sealed, it is not unusual for several gallons of water to accumulate in the duct system.

The dampers in the diffusers can be closed, but if they do not fit tightly, it may be necessary to seal them with plastic. Air from the air conditioning return air system can bulge or even blow out a sealed damper. The return air system can be effectively closed by removing the air filter, putting it in a plastic bag, and reinstalling it.

Hal Handy

Kitchen/Bath

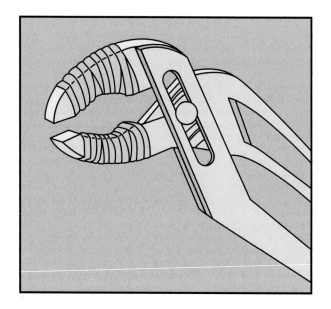

Prevent Scratches on Fixtures

When using Channel Locks or regular pliers on bathroom fixtures, wrap heavy-duty rubber bands around the jaws before tackling the job. The rubber should keep the tool from slipping. No rag can do that. And it will keep the tools from scratching the surface.

George Cole
Sequim, Washington

Preserve a Used Tube of Caulk for Reuse

Preserving a partially used tube of caulk has challenged nearly every do-it-yourselfer.

Home Interiors pg 44

Toilet Touchdown

If you have ever set a toilet, you probably know that it can be difficult to line up the mounting holes with the short bolts on the flange. Next time, slip straws over the bolts to serve as extenders. Then lower the stool using the uprights as guides. The bolts will thread the two holes every time.

Joseph Wang,
Virginia Beach, Virginia

Help Your House Breath When Airing It Out

A range hood, particularly the downdraft type found in newer open grill stoves, can combine with other ventilation systems to cause a backdraft in a home. When the range hood is running in combination with a clothes dryer, bathroom vent, or other ventilation system, it may expel so much air the house is forced to draft air in through a fireplace, furnace, or gas water heater. This can make these appliances smoke, or worse yet, allow potentially deadly carbon monoxide to build up in the home. If a window is opened slightly to provide an air supply for all the ventilation appliances, the problem is eliminated.

Hal Handy

Screw-On Tips Solve Dried Out Caulk

Of the various methods for sealing a partially used tube of caulk, this is one of the easiest and most airtight. Use a large electrical wire nut on the end of the caulk tube tip. Not only do wire nuts prevent the caulk from drying out, you can match the size of the wire nut to the size of the opening you cut on the tip.

Lyle Guion
Lakeland, Florida

Smooth Caulk with Ice

When the instructions on a tube of caulk suggest smoothing the caulk bead with a wet finger, use an ice cube. The ice can be shaped in a few minutes with the heat of your hand, and the water film on the surface of the cube will produce a smooth joint. The caulk can be removed from the ice easily and this smoothing tool just melts away.

Hal Handy

Cure Bathroom Vent Drip

Water often drips from the bathroom vent fan during the winter and can cause paint peeling on the grill, not to mention cold drops on your head. Reducing the problem is a multiple step process. First, be sure that there is a duct attached to the fan so the air is not just blowing into the attic. The fan and housing should then be completely covered with insulation so that the metal housing does not get cold enough to let moisture condense. Next, the duct leading from the fan to the outside should be insulated to reduce condensation in the duct. The fan should be allowed to run a minimum of 15 minutes after showering to remove the humidity and to re-evaporate any moisture that had condensed in the duct. A time switch on the fan makes this more convenient.

Hal Handy

Remove Contact Cement from Your Skin

When using contact cement for attaching plastic laminates, veneers and other thin materials, it is easy to get the cement where it doesn't belong, including your hands. After it dries, a crepe rubber stick, used for cleaning sanding belts, will roll the cement right off without damaging the surface or your skin.

Hal Handy

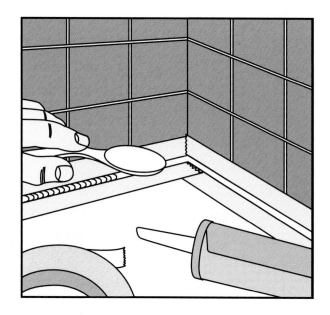

Caulk with Tape

The secret for making a professional looking caulk joint is using painter's tape or masking tape along both sides of the bead. Set the tape along both sides of the joint as far apart as the size of the bead will be. After filling the area, smooth the caulk with a wet finger or plastic caulk spreader. (Plastic horseshoe shims–used for leveling out shoes on a horse–work even better if you can find them.) Remove the painter's tape and you should have a professional looking caulk joint. If removing the tape lifted a corner of the caulk bead, just smooth it down again. There won't be enough excess caulk to spread and spoil the lines.

Jim Drayton
Grandville, Michigan

Adjust the Set-up Time on Caulk

If you want to slow down the curing time of silicone caulk, mist the bead with mineral spirits. To speed up the set-up time, mist the bead with water. Mineral spirits keep hydrogen away from the caulk and slows the curing process. Water adds hydrogen to it.

Michael Haney
Owensville, Montana

Simple Back Draft Damper

The backdraft dampers on kitchen range hoods and bathroom vent fans often don't seal tightly. A no-cost, remarkably effective damper is as near as the produce department of your supermarket. Take a thin, but sturdy, plastic bag, such as stores provide for vegetables and fruits and cut off the bottom to make it into a tube. Disassemble the duct work near the fan in an area where the duct is horizontal, or nearly so. Stuff the open-ended plastic tube into the duct, with the open ends in the direction of the air flow. At the end of the duct, farthest from the fan, attach the bottom edge of the bag to the bottom of the duct with a piece of, what else, duct tape. The other end is cuffed around the joint and the duct reassembled. When the fan is running, the plastic tube will inflate and allow the air to pass through it. When the fan is off and a breeze tries to blow back through the duct, the plastic collapses on itself, sealing the duct tighter than all but the best dampers. The tape on the far end keeps the plastic from being blown backward into the fan.

Hal Handy

An Upright Chain Stops Leaking Toilet Flapper

One reason toilets leak is that the flapper valve doesn't seat well against the drain. This is often caused by the lift chain becoming trapped between the flapper valve and the drain, which prevents the valve from seating properly. To avoid this problem, cut a plastic straw in half. Disconnect the chain and feed it through the straw before reconnecting. Then slide the straw to the bottom of the chain. This will keep the chain from falling to the bottom of the tank and getting caught beneath the valve.

Handyman Club Staff

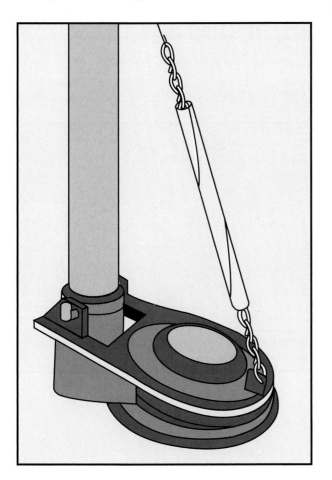

Break Bread to Solder Wet Pipes

When repairing copper pipe it's important to have no water in the pipe when you solder a fitting. To keep water from draining into the section of pipe you're working on, fill the pipe with soft bread. The bread will temporarily absorb the water to allow the fitting to heat and accept the solder. When finished, the soggy bread can be flushed by the water pressure to an open faucet.

Elmer Weaver
Milton, Florida

New (and Less Toxic) Use for Disposable Diapers

Keep a package of disposable diapers handy for emergency leaks and spills around the house. Sometimes, it's not practical to get a bucket under a leaky pipe until you can fix it. Those diapers will hold much more liquid than most people–excepting young parents–would guess.

Richard Orlowsk
New Lisbon, Wisconsin

Plumbing

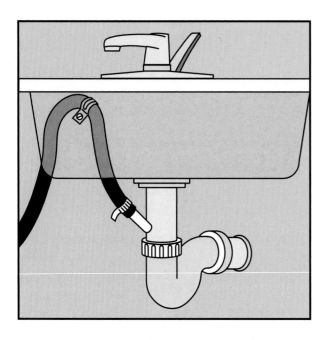

Loop Dishwasher Drain Lines

If the drain line for a dishwasher is connected to a garbage disposer or to a "Y" fitting in the sink drain pipe, the drain line should loop up to top of the sink base before connecting to the disposer or drain. If this is not done, water from the sink can back up into the dishwasher when a full sink is drained. This could contaminate clean dishes in the dishwasher and is unsanitary.

Hal Handy

Don't Hose Freezeproof Faucets in Winter

"Freezeproof" hose faucets may not be freezeproof if a hose is left attached to the faucet in cold weather. This type of faucet operates by locating the actual valve 8-10 inches inside the house. The distance from the valve to the hose threads is really just a pipe. The faucet is designed to have the water drain from the valve to the outside so there is no water to freeze in the cold part of the faucet. A freezeproof faucet with a hose attached may or may not drain. If it doesn't drain, it is more likely to burst than a standard hose faucet–one that should be turned off elsewhere in the house.

Hal Handy

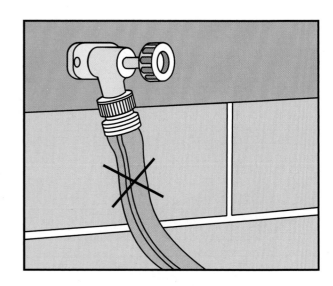

On the Ball Prevents Sewer Gas

Sewer gases can leak into your home and pose health hazards even if you don't detect a strong odor. One of the most common paths for the noxious fumes is through a basement floor drain trap that evaporates dry. Drop an old tennis ball into the drain basin. The ball will seal the opening when it is dry. When water does enter the drain, the ball will float out of the way.

Michael Lehman
Wichita, Kansas

Stop Those Banging Water Pipes

An air chamber, plumbed into a home's water supply lines, reduces a water hammer (the banging sound when a faucet is closed quickly) and helps prevent pipes from bursting if they freeze. Many homes have them. The plumbing system in a house with one or more air chambers should be drained every year or two to allow chambers to refill with air. Air dissolves in water and the air chambers eventually become filled with water, defeating their purpose.

Hal Handy

Sealing the Joint Between the Wall and a Bathtub

When sealing the joint between a bathtub and the adjoining wall, fill the tub with water before caulking. Leave the water in the tub until the caulk sets. The weight of the water will cause the floor framing to sag slightly and the caulk to be compressed when the tub is drained. If the caulking is done with the tub empty, the added weight when in use will stretch the caulk and eventually pull it loose from either the tile or tub.

Hal Handy

Quick Relief for Ceramic Tile Repairs

To remove ceramic tiles to make plumbing repairs, use a Dremel Moto-tool fitted with a .015-.025-thick 1½-inch diameter cut-off disk. Carefully grind away the grout between the tiles. This relieves the pressure between the tiles so that adjacent tiles aren't chipped when an individual tile is removed. Be sure to wear safety goggles.

Gary Howe
Jacksonville, Florida

Walls

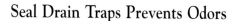
Drywall

Seal Drain Traps Prevents Odors

Drain traps rely on standing water to prevent odors from entering the home from waste pipes. Traps that dry out and lose their seal through lack of use can be a source of odors that are difficult to find. If you have any traps that are used only occasionally (basement floor drains are regular culprits), pour a cup of mineral oil into the drain. It will seal the trap because the oil will not evaporate. If some water does enter the trap, the oil will just be washed into the sewer system. Vegetable oil should not be used, because it can rot and cause an odor worse than the sewer.

Hal Handy

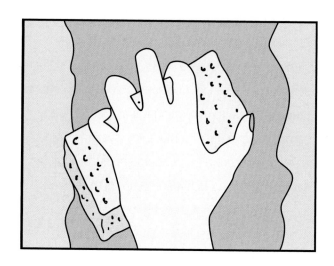

Why Do You Think They Call It Mud?

Here is a great tip for patching, taping, or repairing drywall with joint compound. After the patch or seam is dry, take a damp household sponge to do the finish work, instead of a sander. This does away with all the dust and is much simpler, easier and cheaper to use.

Thomas L. Gaston Sr.
Susana Knolls, California

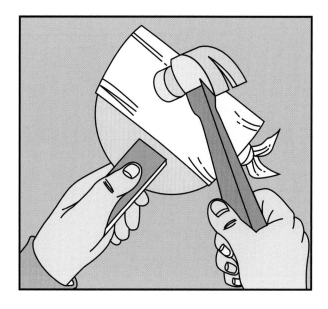

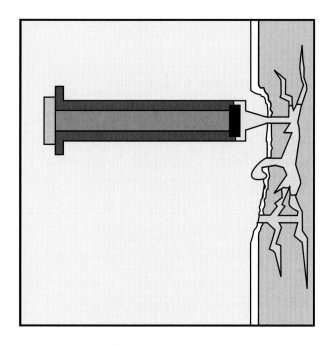

Repair Drywall Cracks

Sometimes, a doorknob gets slammed into
a veneer plaster wall, despite the doorstop, and
will leave a dent. A drywall patch to restore the
strength of the wall can be a major project. The
strength of the backer can be restored by drilling
a series of 3/16-inch holes nearly through the
gypsum board about a half inch apart. Then inject
yellow woodworker's glue into each hole until it
comes out the adjoining hole. Glue injection
syringes are available in most woodworking stores
or catalogs. Let it dry overnight. Then fill the
remainder of the dent with spackling.

Hal Handy

Popping Popped Nails Back In

Before digging out the compound and refilling,
priming, and painting a nail pop in drywall, try this
first. Place a wide putty knife or wall knife, wrapped
in a single thickness of cloth, such as a handkerchief,
over the nail and give it a sharp hit with a hammer.
The knife spreads the force of the blow to keep
from damaging the drywall, and the nail is
knocked back into place.

Hal Handy

Remember Your Paint Colors for Later Reference

After painting a room, write the date, brand of
paint, color name or number, finish style (flat, satin
or semi-gloss), etc., on a piece of masking tape
and affix it to the back of the light switch cover.

Michael Haney
Owensville, Montana

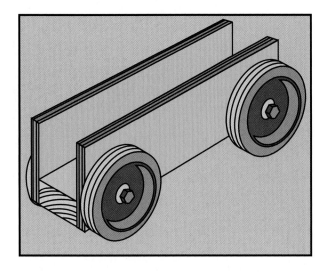

Utility Cart for Moving Plywood or Drywall

A small cart with wheels makes moving plywood or drywall around the shop or at a remodeling site much easier. Get four 6-inch replacement lawnmower wheels and two 8-inch long ½-inch fully threaded carriage bolts and eight nuts. Cut the head off the bolts to serve as axles. Two nuts on each end will secure the wheels. Tentatively assemble the axles to measure the distance between the two wheels, when they're thrust to each end. The cart body is a length of 2"x4" about 18 inches long, laid flat. The sides are about 3 inches high and made of at least ½-inch plywood. Depending on what you use for the sides, the 2x4 should be ripped to a width so that the assembled body is ¼-inch narrower than the space between the wheels on the assembled axles. The sides are attached to the body with screws and some yellow glue. The axle holes are bored through the sides of the body a few inches from each end. The wheels and axles are assembled to the body, and the two nuts at the end of each axle tightened against each so they

don't come loose. Peen the ends of the axles so they don't cut either woodwork or ankles. Add a few drops of oil, and the cart is ready to roll.

Hal Handy

Simple Dry Wall Kicker

A drywall "kicker" is used to raise and hold the bottom sheet of drywall up against the top sheet without squeezing your fingers. If you sometimes have to hang a sheet or two of drywall, but not enough to justify owning a kicker, try making this tool out of a flat prybar, such as the Wonderbar. Drill a pilot hole for a #10 sheet metal screw in the side of a 3-inch piece of conduit. Then push the screw through the oval-shaped, nail-pulling slot of the flat prybar and attach the conduit. Tightening the screw to lock the conduit at a 90-degree angle to the pry bar. The conduit serves as a fulcrum for

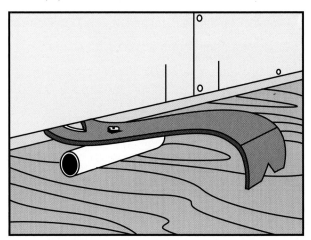

the prybar so the toe of the bar can lift the drywall about two inches with a little pressure from your foot on the hooked end.

Hal Handy

No Fuss, No Mess Drilling in Plaster

Here's how to avoid dust on your rugs and furniture when you're drilling through drywall, plaster or any other wall board. First, mark the wall where you're going to drill. Take a long business-style envelope, fold the flap back and tape it to the wall about an inch under the point you're going to drill. Drill the hole with one hand and pull the envelope open with the other hand. The dust from the drilling falls right into the envelope, avoiding the usual mess. Remove the envelope, seal it and toss it. There's no mess, no dust and no need to vacuum.

John Whitaker
Everett, Massachusetts

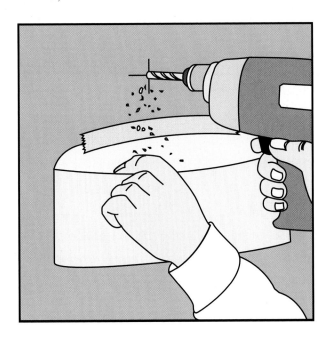

He's Got Buckets On the Soles of His Shoes

A quick and easy substitute for drywall stilts is to make your own. For small jobs, screw an old pair of shoes to the bottoms of two empty drywall compound buckets. Put a piece of plywood in the bottom of the buckets to give your screws something to bite. Carefully put your feet in the shoes and stand up. This will raise you about 15 inches. That will give you the necessary reach for most drywall or other jobs in rooms with eight-foot ceilings. They are clunky, and you have to go through doorways sideways, but they work surprisingly well.

Hal Handy

53

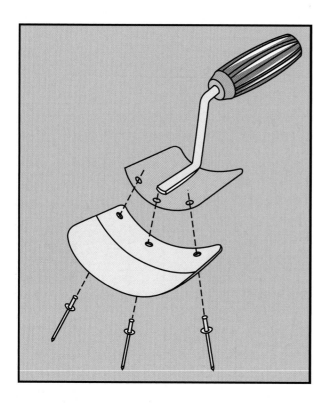

Flexible Trowel Works on Angled Joints

Here's how to make a flexible trowel for applying drywall joint compound to seams of varying angles, besides a regular 90-degree angle. Use a 3½"x6¼" plastic putty spreader (used in bodyshop for auto repair putty, etc.) and a medium sized concrete trowel. Cut off the pointed end of the trowel with a hack saw. Leave about two inches just enough room to attach to the plastic spreader.

Bend the remainder of flat surface of the trowel to the approximate angle you need to work with. Attach the flexible putty spreader with a pop rivet at each outer edge so that it is cupped when it's attached. The flexible front of the plastic spreader will form itself to fit the contour or angle of your seams and allows good control of the spreader.

George F. Smith
Orange, Connecticut

Budget Drywall Ceiling Helper

Installing drywall on the ceiling is usually a two person job because the 4'x8' sheets of drywall are heavy, clumsy and fragile. If you have to work alone, this is one way to hang a drywall ceiling. Starting in a corner, attach 2"x4"s flat against the studs of both walls about 1 inch below the ceiling joists. Lift the edge of the first drywall panel into the shelf formed by one 2"x4" and then slide it into the shelf formed by the other 2"x4". After making sure your free corner is centered on the joist, start driving drywall screws. For subsequent pieces, reposition one 2"x4", nailing it again to the wall studs. Lay the other 2"x4" flat over the edge of the drywall you've just secured and screw through the drywall into the joist, leaving a 1-inch wide shelf for the next sheet of drywall. The cost of these "helpers" is the price of a couple of 2"x4"s.

Ken Althoff
Holley, New York

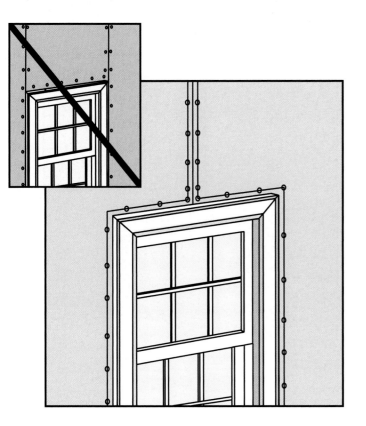

Drywall Around Windows and Doors

When hanging drywall, never place joints flush with sides of windows or doors. Due to moisture in the air and the expansion that can occur next to doors and windows, the joints will eventually crack. Move joints away from windows where you can. Where you can't, butt the joint with large sheets at least 6 inches away from the edge of the door or window.

Charles Van de Riet
Landrum, South Carolina

Finishing

Glue and Cross Nailing Holds Curved Trim

Sometimes it is necessary to nail a piece of trim to a curved wall. Frequently, there is no solid backing for the drywall or plaster on these curved sections. A nail driven straight into the wallboard will pull out easily. Driving a pair of nails at opposing angles will hold much better. Combined with a few spots of construction adhesive–not too much to make removing the trim a chore–will keep these pieces in place as long as you want.

Hal Handy

Remove Wallpaper Paste

If wallpaper paste is not completely removed from a wall to be painted, the paint will probably "alligator"–leave thin cracks in the paint. A quick way of removing the dried-on paste is to apply a thin coat of drywall compound. Let it set for 15 minutes, then scrape the compound and the paste off the wall. The moisture in the taping compound loosens the paste and the compound serves as a vehicle to carry the paste off the wall. If the compound dries too hard before you get to it, dampen it with a wet cloth. The wall should then be washed with tri-sodium phosphate (TSP) to remove anything remaining on the wall. Drywall compound that has frozen and cannot be used for permanent walls works fine for paste removal.

Hal Handy

Trimming Tips Save Time and Effort

Most handymen know to dull the tip of a finish nail to avoid splitting trim pieces, but here's a refinement on that technique. Put the head of the nail against the trim piece where you intend to drive it. When you tap the nail point to dull it, you simultaneously create a countersunk pilot dimple. For easy sinking, then dip the nail point in beeswax, which you can keep in a drilled-out cavity in the handle of your trim hammer.

Fritz Korte
Pacific, Montana

Remove Paint from Screw Heads

It is difficult to remove a screw when the slot is clogged with paint. Tighten a 4d finishing nail into the chuck of a small or medium drill. Put the point of the nail in the paint-filled slot and use it like a router to clear out enough paint to make room for the screwdriver tip. It works with either slotted or Phillips screw heads. When the corners of the nail become rounded off, you can replace it, or it can be quickly sharpened with a few swipes of a file.

Hal Handy

Use Foam Painters for Staining

A foam pad painter works better than a brush for many staining jobs. It holds more stain, drips less, and the amount of stain applied can be regulated by the amount of pressure applied. The stain can be applied to the pad with a squeeze bottle to avoid having to clean up the roller or other pan.

Hal Handy

Prepare Interior Woodwork for Paint

Sometimes interior woodwork is too rough to repaint but not bad enough to require stripping. A sheet of wet-or-dry sandpaper, a firm sponge, a scrub brush, and a bucket of water will help recondition the surface. Wrap the sandpaper around the sponge and wet them both. Use it as though it was a flexible sanding block. Scrubbing the paper with the brush in the bucket will make it last a long time. The water traps the particles of dried paint rather than releasing them into the air. This is important because the paint could be lead-based and therefore a health hazard. The sandpaper will feather out any rough edges but still leave enough tooth to hold the paint. This also works for wet sanding cars after painting. The sponge flexes to allow for contour of the body.

Handyman Club Staff

Wall Miscellaneous

Ceiling Mildew a Sign of Poor Insulation

Mildew spots on the ceiling at an outside wall are usually caused by a lack of insulation on the top of the wall. Frequently this is caused when air, moving through the soffit vents into the attic, has blown the insulation back away from the wall. Install permanent plastic air chutes between each rafter. These chutes will allow the air to flow from the soffit into the attic without raising the end of the insulation batts or blowing loose fill insulation back from the edge. If needed, fold a small batt of insulation and stuff it between the chute and the top of the wall. If the insulation has been blown around, push it back into place with a rake.

Hal Handy

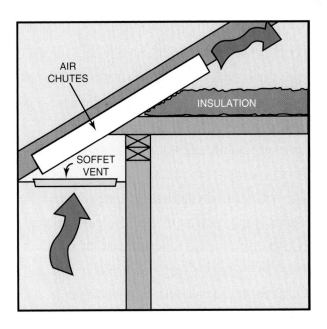

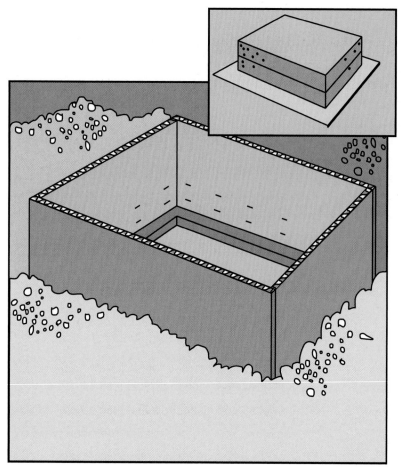

Insulate An Attic Scuttle Cover

The attic scuttle cover—that little removable board that allows access to the attic crawlspace–is not often insulated, The explanation is simple: Even though the rest of the attic is well insulated, the cover was not in place when the insulator did his job. The best way to insulate an attic scuttle cover is to surround the opening with a dam about a foot high. This dam can be made out of scrap plywood. Hold it in place with a few nails. The scuttle cover should be ½-inch gypsum drywall glued to ½-inch plywood to resist breaking. To the back of the cover attach 2 to 4 inches of expanded foam board insulation. This thickness can be layers of thinner material. The first layer should be attached with construction adhesive and shingle nails. The other layers should be glued and nailed, if possible. The dam keeps dust and insulation from falling out of the attic when the cover is lifted.

Hal Handy

Dark Streaks on Ceilings

A dark streak that appears on a ceiling is usually dust that has been captured by a microscopic film of moisture condensing on the plaster because the ceiling insulation doesn't fit tightly. Most often, these streaks appear at or near a ceiling joist. The streaks will wash off, but they will return unless the insulation batts are pushed tightly against the ceiling joists or a layer of loose fill insulation is added over the insulation batts to fill the cracks between the batts. A larger dark area usually indicates that some insulation is missing or is out of position for some reason.

Hal Handy

Home Interior Miscellaneous

Slick, Quick Batt Cuts

To cut kraft-faced fiberglass batt insulation, use this technique. Lay the insulation paper-side down on a piece of scrap plywood. Then lay a 1"x6" board on top of the insulation along the cutting line. Step on the 1"x6" and, with a utility knife, cut the compressed insulation with a single pass.

Steve Lacey
Boston, Massachusetts

The Easy Clean Way for Air Conditioner Drains

To keep your central air conditioner and basement floor drain flowing all year long, pour liquid household bleach into the air conditioner's condenser drain tube midway through the cooling season and treat the floor drain at least monthly. Otherwise slimy bacteria will clog the line and drain.

Stewart Simmons
Washington, D.C.

Coffee Filter Plucker

Do you have trouble removing just one coffee filter at a time from the package? It's unsanitary to lick your fingers to give them enough tack to pluck out the filter. Try the magic Coffee Filter Plucker (CFP) instead.

Cut a 3" long piece of masking tape and fold it back on itself about 1". Hold the folded back portion of the tape between your thumb and forefinger. Tap the sticky side to the coffee filter, and you will pluck out one at a time without fail. Leave the CFP in the box or bag of filters for the next time.

Each CFP will last about one month before it wears out. One roll of masking tape will make enough CFPs to last a lifetime.

James J. Myers
West Los Angeles, California

Getting His Fill Of Coffee

Here's the start to a fresh day. Run a water supply line to your under-the-cabinet coffee maker. Run a ½" copper supply line to an area under the cabinet just to the side of the coffee maker and install a standard chrome bathroom shutoff valve there. Then run a flexible ⅜ inch copper tube from the shutoff and bend it down into the coffee maker's water reservoir. All you have to do is open the shutoff to fill the water reservoir.

Therian Marshall
Martinsville, Virginia

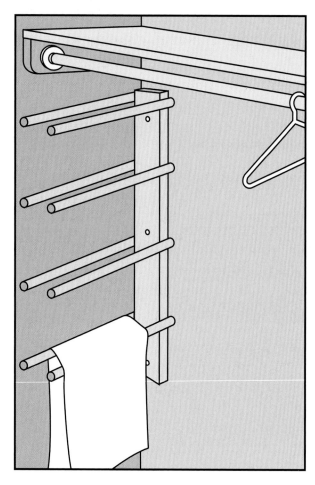

Out Of Sight, But Not Sound

Stereo speakers should be heard but their wires should not be seen. To keep the cables from being an eyesore and a safety hazard, tuck them out of sight between the baseboard molding and the nailing strips used to hold in wall-to-wall carpeting. Use a blunt, but narrow object such as a wooden paint stirrer or putty knife to push the wires in place without damaging them.

Linn Bergmann
Plymouth, Minnesota

Store Large Tablecloths

Storing large tablecloths can be a problem because the more you fold them, the more they tend to crease. Because large table clothes are usually used for company, that means ironing them before using them. A solution is to find a corner in a nearby closet and install a 1" dowel, like an additional closet rod, on one side of the closet. You can install additional poles approximately 12 to 15 inches higher or lower so that you can hang several tablecloths in the same closet. This will minimize wrinkling and creasing of your tablecloths between uses. You can also install a shelf above the top pole where you can store napkins and other dining room accessories.

Handyman Club Staff

SHOP

- Projects
- Tools
- Woodworking
- Shop Miscellaneous

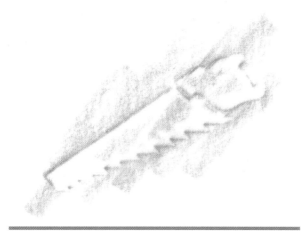

Shop Projects

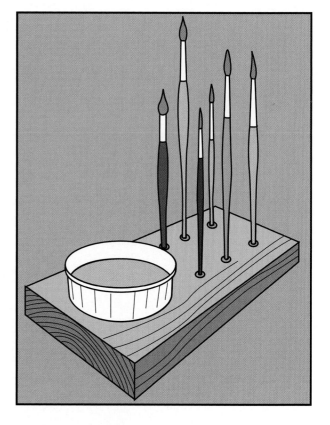

Avoid Ugly Stained Plywood

Most people who have stained pine or fir plywood were unhappy with the results. Plywood doesn't take dark stains evenly and even a little smoothing with steel wool is sometimes enough to rub through the stain. There is nothing wrong with painting plywood, because a good looking paint job is better than a poor staining one. If you must stain, condition the wood with linseed oil which will make the wood absorb the stain evenly. Then use one of the Danish oil stains and put a wax finish on it. If the project is going outside, use a semi-transparent outdoor stain.

Jeremy Powers
Fridley, Minnesota

Rack for Small Brushes

Small paint brushes are hard to store. Build a holder for them out of scrap lumber. Drill various sizes of holes to accept a variety of handles. This way, your brushes are stored upright and the rack is easily carried to each project. Put a 2" hole near one corner for disposable cups. They'll be less likely to spill.

John J. Williams
Paulsboro, New Jersey

Mix Small Quantities of Glue

Plastic measuring cups from cough medicine or cold remedies are excellent for mixing small quantities of epoxy adhesives and two-part waterproof glues. Oftentimes they're graduated, so you can accurately mix equal amounts. When the unused material in the cup is dry, it's an indicator that epoxy or glue is sufficiently set on your project and can be safely handled. No clean up is required. Simply throw the cup away!

Stephen J. Sabo
Cleveland, Ohio

Spray Foam that Doesn't Quit

When using do-it-yourself cans of expanding urethane spray foam, always have an empty bucket nearby. Occasionally, a valve on these cans will stick open, and a continuous stream of what must be one of the world's stickiest materials can create a huge mess. Putting the erupting can in a bucket so that it can be safely carried outside will greatly reduce the mess you have to clean up.

Hal Handy

Waxing Prophetically about Tape Edges

Spraying the sides of a roll of duct tape with a spray wax or silicone will keep those sticky edges from collecting dirt, paper and even staples. Spraying the edges of a roll of masking tape or rubbing it with a wax block, candle or crayon will reduce the chance of pulling up the paint film when the tape is removed.

Hal Handy

Turn an Antique Wood Dresser Into a Vanity

A creative project that adds a distinctive touch to your home's bathroom–especially if you decorate with antique furniture and accessories–is to mount a bathroom sink in an antique dresser instead of a commercial vanity. Such an unusual project will bring many comments from friends and neighbors and make your bathroom unique.

1. Begin scouting antique and secondhand furniture stores and garage sales for a suitable old dresser. Size and shape, as well as cost and condition, will be the deciding factors. If the top drawer does not slide well, that's okay. It will be sealed shut to accommodate the sink and drain pipe within the dresser. And, if you are lucky enough to find a dresser that has a matching mirror, all the better.

The mirror and frame can be mounted on the wall over the dresser at the appropriate height for personal grooming.

2. Next visit your local plumbing supply store or lumberyard to find a bathroom sink that will fit into the dresser you selected. You can also use an old sink. Factors to consider are your price range, how the sink will look when installed and how much refinishing it will need. Buy a set of lavatory handles and faucet that will coordinate with the appearance of the old dresser.

3. Make any repairs to the dresser, mirror and frame, if necessary. Because it will be near water, it will need two coats of modern polyurethane varnish. If the finish is in good shape, you can apply it over the existing finish. If the dresser's finish isn't intact, refinish the whole dresser. Remove the drawer front of the top drawer. The front will be installed after the sink has been installed. The second drawer should also be removed and altered to accommodate the drain pipe. One solution is to make a U-shaped cut in the middle of the back of the drawer. This will allow it to be used as storage but will slide in and out of the dresser around the drain pipe.

4. Trace the shape of the hole to be cut on the top of dresser using the diagram of the sink dimension that comes with all new sinks. If an old sink is used its size and overall shape will determine the dimension of the hole. With a jig-saw, cut the hole for the sink from the top of the dresser. Depending on the shape of the dresser, an oval sink usually looks best and is easier to install.

5. Set and tightly fasten the sink into place on the dresser. Position the dresser against the wall in your bathroom and screw the dresser into the studs of the wall. It may be necessary to remove part of the back of the dresser, but leave as much as you can. Hook up the water lines and drain pipe as called for in the instructions that came with the sink and hardware.

6. Glue the top drawer front into place and insert the next drawer. Slide the second drawer in and make any final modifications so that it fits around the water lines and drain pipe. Open each water facet to check that they work properly and to detect any leaks. Also open and close the drain to ascertain that it is working correctly.

7. Depending on the height of the dresser, the matching frame and mirror can be mounted on top or directly above it to the wall. Most old dresser mirrors will be too low if set on top of the dresser, so consider screwing the mirror frame directly to the wall. If the surface is drywall, use plastic anchors in the wall to secure the mirror.

Consider installing ceramic tile between the dresser top and the mirror frame to protect the drywall from water damage. This is also an attractive addition if you've used tile elsewhere in the bathroom.

This project makes a unique decorative statement to your home without spending much money. It's a fairly simply project and can produce big results.

Jay Black
Clear Lake, Iowa

Adirondack chair

A great use for wood scraps from a deck or picnic table project, the Adirondack chair is a prefect compliment to your main construction. Since the wood from these outdoor projects is usually pressure treated, use caution when working with it and in its disposal. Begin by making cardboard, hardboard or plywood templates of the chair's rear legs, arms and seat-back slats. The time you invest in making these templates is well-spent because it allows you to refine the profiles on the template material rather than wasting usable stock. Templates also make it easy to move the shapes around on the lengths of lumber to avoid defects such as knots or holes. Once the templates are ready, trace the leg, arm and back slat profiles onto the appropriate blanks. Then use either a saber saw, a jig saw or a band saw to cut out the shapes. Stay on the waste side of the layout lines as you make the cuts, then use a file to smooth the newly cut surfaces and remove the marks left by the saw blade. Tip: Filing usually works better than sanding because of the high moisture content of new pressure-treated wood.

Cut the remaining chair parts to finished size, using either a table saw or hand-held circular saw and a speed-square for a guide.

To prevent splinters, use a ¼-in. rounding-over bit in a router to ease the sharp edges on all chair parts before assembly.

Lay out the location of the 2"x4" rear rail on the curved rear leg, then fasten it in place between the legs, using 12d galvanized nails and construction adhesive. Adhere and nail the front seat rail to the ends of the rear legs, leaving an overhang of 2¾-in. at each end for the front legs.

Temporarily clamp the front legs in position so you can drill pilot holes through the front rail and into the legs; then apply adhesive to the joints and secure them with 2-in. galvanized deck screws. Drill pilot holes for attaching the seat boards, then apply adhesive and install the boards, again using 2-in. screws.

Next, place the backrest boards together on the workbench, with their backside facing up. Position the backrest stretcher over the boards and drill pilot holes through the stretcher and into the slats. Then, apply construction adhesive and screw the stretcher to the boards. Slide the back assembly into place on the chair, drill pilot holes and attach the boards with construction adhesive and screws.

Finally, position the arms on the chair and attach them. Use screws to fasten the back of the arms but 12d galvanized nails to secure the front of the arms to the end grain of the front legs.

When the chair is sufficiently dry (less than 18-percent moisture content), seal and finish the surfaces.

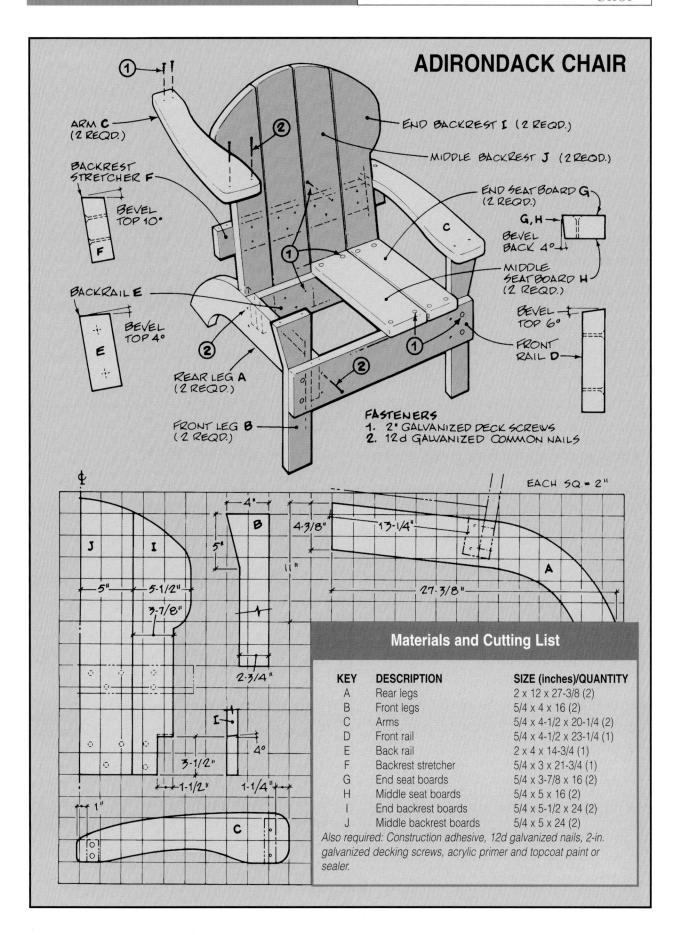

ADIRONDACK CHAIR

ARM **C**
(2 REQD.)

BACKREST
STRETCHER **F**

BEVEL
TOP 10°

F

BACKRAIL **E**

BEVEL
TOP 4°

E

REAR LEG **A**
(2 REQD.)

FRONT LEG **B**
(2 REQD.)

END BACKREST **I** (2 REQD.)

MIDDLE BACKREST **J** (2 REQD.)

END SEAT BOARD **G**
(2 REQD.)

G, H

BEVEL
BACK 4°

MIDDLE
SEAT BOARD **H**
(2 REQD.)

BEVEL
TOP 6°

FRONT
RAIL **D**

C

FASTENERS
1. 2" GALVANIZED DECK SCREWS
2. 12d GALVANIZED COMMON NAILS

EACH SQ.= 2"

4"

B

5"

4-3/8"

13-1/4"

11"

A

J   **I**

5"   5-1/2"

3-7/8"

27-3/8"

I

4°

3-1/2"

1-1/2"   1-1/4"

2-3/4"

1"

C

Materials and Cutting List

KEY	DESCRIPTION	SIZE (inches)/QUANTITY
A	Rear legs	2 x 12 x 27-3/8 (2)
B	Front legs	5/4 x 4 x 16 (2)
C	Arms	5/4 x 4-1/2 x 20-1/4 (2)
D	Front rail	5/4 x 4-1/2 x 23-1/4 (1)
E	Back rail	2 x 4 x 14-3/4 (1)
F	Backrest stretcher	5/4 x 3 x 21-3/4 (1)
G	End seat boards	5/4 x 3-7/8 x 16 (2)
H	Middle seat boards	5/4 x 5 x 16 (2)
I	End backrest boards	5/4 x 5-1/2 x 24 (2)
J	Middle backrest boards	5/4 x 5 x 24 (2)

Also required: Construction adhesive, 12d galvanized nails, 2-in. galvanized decking screws, acrylic primer and topcoat paint or sealer.

Using a straight edge, make the cuts starting with the seat support. Use a straight edge for as many cuts as you can. Work your way down the sheet of plywood, following the diagram and cutting each part. Wait until all parts are cut out before cutting notches and the recesses on the seat supports and the cross brace.

A Portable Picnic Table from One Sheet of Plywood

This is a plan for a small picnic table that is easily assembled and disassembled without tools or hardware. It's great if you've ever wanted an extra picnic table for entertaining, but didn't want to have to store it. And it's a sturdy portable table to take camping or on vacation, and it doesn't cost a lot. This is a 2'x4' picnic table, cut from one sheet of plywood. When disassembled, it measures just 29" by 48" by less than 3. It seats four adults, although it's a little low for long-term seating. But it easily seats six kids.

Lightly sketch the cutting diagram on your plywood sheet. You'll need a circular saw with a sharp plywood blade and an electric jig saw with a sharp, hollow-ground fine blade. The plywood should be at least AC grade.

All notches should be ¾" to accept other parts of the plywood. If you plan to paint the finished project, cut them an extra ¹⁄₁₆" wider. The friction of the notches in the end of the seats and the table top are all that hold those pieces in place so don't cut them too wide.

If you have a table saw, use it to cut the long recesses on the tops of the seat supports and the cross brace. The seats and the table top will rest on these. If the cuts are wavy, the seats or top could rock. To do this, set your table saw fence for ¾", less the width of the saw blade. Drop the blade below the surface of the table. Put the plywood piece on the table saw so that the 3" notch is just past the blade by about another 3 inches. Start the saw and raise the saw blade until it cuts through and just rises above the plywood. Push the plywood along until about six inches from the other end. Finish the cuts with a jig saw.

Once all the parts are cut, finish the table. You can paint, use an outdoor stain or varnish. For a fancier table, you can veneer the edges, seats and the top slanted parts of the sides.

To assemble the table, stand one of the sides up so that it looks a like an "A" and slide one of the long notches of the cross brace into the long center slot of the side. Then repeat the procedure with the other side. The table framework will now stand up. Slide the seat supports down into the notches on each side. Slide the seats into the little notches on the sides and fit them over the upright tabs of the seat supports. The table top goes on last by pushing it down over the upright tabs on the cross brace.

Jeremy Powers
Fridley, Minnesota

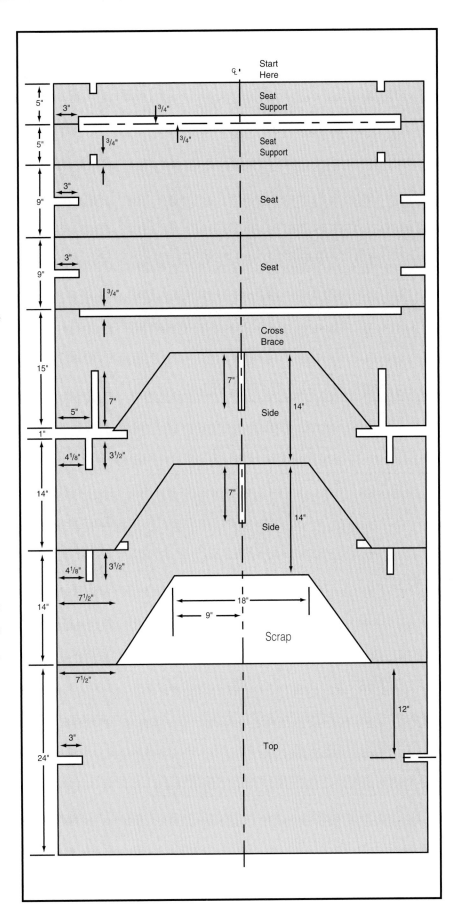

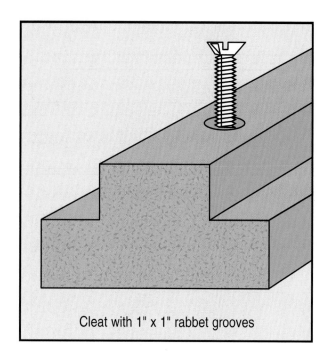

Cleat with 1" x 1" rabbet grooves

Turn a Workmate into a Work Bench

Black and Decker's Workmate is handy mini work bench. But adding a removable top made out of plywood and 2"x4"s makes it more useful.

Use a 2'x4' piece of ¾" plywood for the top. Cut a ¾"x¾" rabbet groove on the edge of a 2"x4"–enough to go all the way around the edge. Miter the corners and make a frame out of the 2"x4"s in which to put the plywood. Fasten the four corners with countersunk screws. Glue and fasten the top with nails. Use a ½" rounding router bit and take the edges off all four top edges and up each of the corners. For fastening the top to the Workmate, build a large cleat out of a 2"x4". Make 1" by 1" rabbet grooves on the two top edges of a 12"–2"x4" laying flat. Using two 2½" flat-head stove bolts, fasten the cleat to the bottom side of the work top. Counter sink the heads of the bolts below the work surface and use washers and nuts on the other side.

To secure the top, tighten the Workmate on the cleat so the two portions of the Workmate top clamp into the two grooves of the 2"x4" cleat.

Jeremy Powers
Fridley, Minnesota

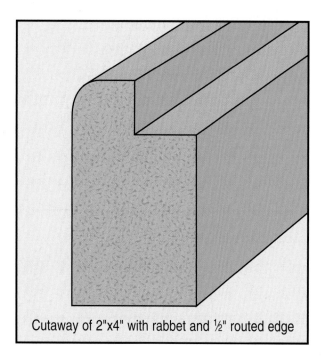

Cutaway of 2"x4" with rabbet and ½" routed edge

Remove Oil Stains from Your Hands

Although oil stains can be removed from your hands with mineral spirits and scrubbing them with detergent, I found that salad oil will dilute the stain and allow you to wipe it off your hands. I carry a bottle of cheap olive oil and find that this will lift most oil stains off skin without solvents, many of which carry a warning against prolonged skin contact. Lanolin-based or citrus-based mechanics hand cleaners will do the same job.

Hal Handy

Clearing Spray Paint Can Nozzles

When using just part of a can of spray paint, the remainder is often wasted because the nozzle becomes clogged with dried paint. Either the clogged nozzle will not work or it will produce a poor, unusable spray pattern. Even nozzles that are cleared by turning the can over and spraying just propellant can clog. A better way is to remove the spray nozzle and put it on a can of WD-40. A couple of squirts and the nozzle will be very clean.

Hal Handy

Clean Foam Spray from Your Hands

The instructions on cans of do-it-yourself expanding urethane foam always recommend using rubber gloves. Despite instructions, some of us are tempted to do small jobs without bothering with the gloves. If you do get some of the foam on your hands, mineral spirits will take it off if used immediately. Automotive carburetor/choke cleaner will take it off easier, as long as it is not more than 10 minutes old. Once it is set, you may have to wear it off.

Hal Handy

Sand End Grain Finer

When working on a project with solid woods in which an end grain will be exposed, always sand the end grain to a finer finish than the rest of the project. If the rest of your project is sanded smooth with 150 grit, go to 220 for the end grain. This will mean the end grain is as smooth as the rest of the project when varnished.

Jeremy Powers
Fridley, Minnesota

Don't Use Steel Wool with Water-Borne Finishes

The environmentally friendly water-borne finishes have become as good as the oil-based ones. But, if you're working on a project that you plan to finish with a water-borne varnish, don't use regular steel wool. Despite all the improvements in these formulas, water still rusts steel and you can get little rusts spots. Use stainless steel, brass or one of the new artificial steel wool pads.

Jeremy Powers
Fridley, Minnesota

Using Urethane Foam

When using cans of expanding urethane foam to seal between the rough opening and the finish frames of doors and windows, it is important to lay a bead of foam only on the inner or outer edge of the space. Even the low-expansion foams can produce enough pressure to bow in the door frames if the full depth of the space is filled. The space can be filled with the traditional fiberglass or with polyethylene foam caulking rope before the foam seal is applied at the inner edge. Allow the foam to set overnight. Use a mastic trowel as a saw to trim the foam flush with the interior finish and jamb.

Hal Handy

Water-Borne Varnishes Won't Darken Wood Color

Water-borne varnishes are remarkably clear–so clear, in fact, that they won't give a project a golden varnish color. That makes them ideal when re-varnishing a project that already is the right color. It also makes water-borne varnish a good choice when varnishing woods that are already dark, such as walnut, butternut, rosewood, ebony, wenge and purpleheart.

Jeremy Powers
Fridley, Minnesota

Remove Stick-On-Labels

Stick-on labels, used by merchants and manufacturers, are intended to be difficult to remove to deter theft. But when they're on a product you have bought, they can be difficult to remove without scratching the surface. Spray the label with oil-like cooking spray or the ever-handy WD-40. The light oil will usually loosen the label in a few minutes. When nothing else is available, you can even use vegetable oil or even spread the label with peanut butter. The natural peanut oil will do the job.

Hal Handy

Ten Safe Inexpensive Tips

These are the 10 safest things you can do in your home to protect against fires, accidents and break–ins.

1. Install a high-quality smoke detector on each level of your home.
2. Install a carbon monoxide detector in or near your utility room or wherever you have an appliance that burns natural gas or wood.
3. Inspect, remove debris and install a cap on every chimney, including the metal ones for furnaces and water heaters.
4. Plan an emergency escape route from every room in your home and make sure everyone knows it.
5. Have a working fire extinguisher in the kitchen and shop and an additional one on each level of your home.
6. If you have glass doors, install a prominent sticker or decal on it at eye level so no one accidentally walks through it.
7. If your bath tub is slippery, install rubber appliques to reduce falling.
8. Have a locksmith inspect, repair and change the key cylinders on all the locks in your home at least once every five years.
9. Install a light fixture with a motion detector to illuminate each entrance to your home.
10. Install a ground fault circuit interrupter (GFCI) receptacle to protect every electrical outlet in the kitchen, bathroom and laundry room.

Jeremy Powers
Fridley, Minnesota

Shop Tools

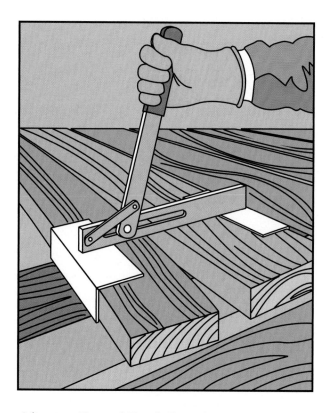

Tighten Those Loose Screws

About once a year, walk around the house with a couple of screw drivers and tighten every screw that you can find. You might be surprised how much a screw can work loose over the course of a year, especially in door hinges and cabinets. This routine maintenance will ensure that everything stays in tip top shape.

Handyman Club Staff

Keep Cords Connected

Although there are numerous products on the market designed to keep two cords plugged in, the easiest and always available method is to tie a loose overhand knot with the two cords and plug them together. Tension on the two cords actually tightens the union so the connection stays together throughout your work.

Handyman Club Staff

Aligning Bowed Deck Boards

A brick tong is a handy tool to pull warped deck boards into alignment. By starting the nail or screw, then using one hand on the lift lever of the tong and the other hand holding the hammer or screw gun, one person can fasten a bowed board into place quickly.

Hal Handy

Repair Padlock Operation

When a padlock becomes stiff or hard to open because of weathering or rust, and graphite fails to loosen it, as a last resort pour a small amount of motor oil in the opening on the top of the lock and in the key hole.

*John Forestiere
Hackettstown, New Jersey*

Plastic Jars for Storage Instead of Glass

Virtually every handyman has stored little parts in baby food jars. Many people use jars because they allow immediate identification of the contents. But the biggest problem is they're made of glass and they can break if dropped or knocked off a work bench. Instead of glass, use clear plastic food jars, such as the ones peanut butter come in. They're a little larger, which means they're great for the storage of screws, nails, small tools, etc. These plastic jars are ideal for tool boxes because they won't spill and they're unbreakable.

Charles Parker
Aurora, Colorado

Plenty of Pencils is a Cheap Way to Avoid Frustration

When working around the shop, a common problem is misplacing your pencil. To avoid the frustration of continuously looking for it, place little tool holders (orange juice cans work well, too) in different spots around your workshop. Put one or two pencils in each one. When you misplace one pencil, you'll still have others handy to choose from. Put out as many as you want as this is a very inexpensive way to avoid frustration.

Donald Robillard
Dartmouth, Massachusetts

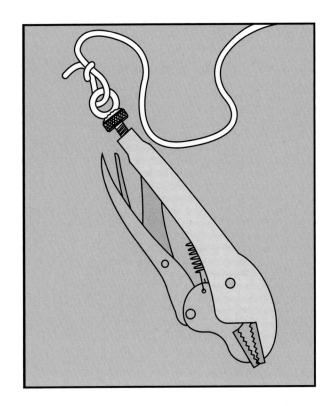

Basic Hoist for Light Material

Bulky but light items, such as flashings, chimney caps, etc., can be hoisted to a roof safely and quickly by welding a ring to the adjusting knob of a pair of Vise-Grip locking pliers. Tie a rope to the ring. Snap the locking pliers onto the object to be hoisted and lift it easily to the roof.

Hal Handy

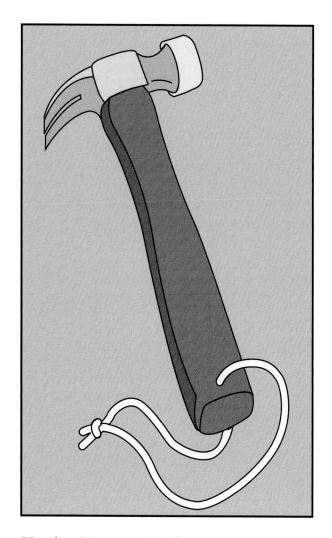

Handier Hammer Handle

Drill a ³⁄₁₆" hole near the end of your hammer handle and loop a 12" piece of nylon cord through it. If you put your wrist through the cord before grabbing the handle, like a ski pole strap, you can let go of the hammer without dropping it. If you ever do drop it into an unreachable area, you can easily recover it. All you would need is a long stick with a wire hook on one end to reach down and grab the cord loop.

Don Mosely
Pacific Grove, California

Sizing Up Your Nail Needs

Here's a way to tell what size nail (4d, 16d, etc.) is right for the job. (It works for nails up to 3 inches long). Determine the length of nail that you need in inches and subtract ½". Then multiply by 4. If you need a nail that is 1½" long, subtract ½", multiply by 4 and what you need is a 4-penny nail.

Handyman Club Staff

Coil Spring Rollers

Using rollers to move heavy objects works well until the roller hits some small obstruction, such as a pebble. Instead of solid rollers, such as old closet rods, you can get a matched set of coil springs from an old car at your local auto salvage yard. These big springs roll better over rough surfaces and because they are hollow, will miss most little obstructions. If it hits one, the round spring will push small objects out of the way.

Hal Handy

Don't Let Power Cords Get You Down

When working in your shop, power cords often get in the way of free movement. They can get caught on the corners of saw horses and work benches. If they're on the floor, you can trip on them. One fix is to suspend them from the ceiling. Hang a long spring from the ceiling with a clip attached to the end. An old-fashioned screen door spring works fine unless the ceiling is very high. Simply clip the tool cord to the end of the spring. One of those six-outlet strips attached to such a spring gives you multiple outlets. The flexibility of the spring means no abrupt jerks and it will keep the cord out of your way.

Tom Beard
Moores Hill, Indiana

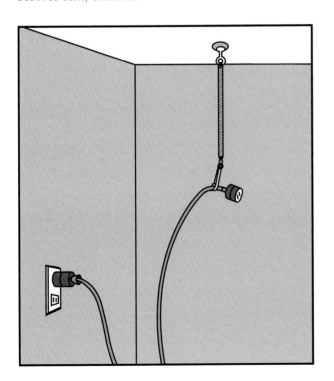

Nail Set Holders

Nail sets are one of those valuable tools that always seem to be misplaced. Using a scrap of wood, you can make a workbench top holder that will keep them convenient. Take a 1½" long piece of 2"x2" clear pine. Place it so the end grain is face up. Using a ¼" bit, drill a 1" deep hole in the center of the turning square. Next, drill four more holes placed at an equal distance from the center hole and each of the corners of the 2"x2". Sand and finish if you'd like. Place your nail sets in the holes with the point down.

Steve Simonton
Tampa, Florida

Blow Sawdust Away

Use an old aquarium air pump to blow sawdust away from the work on your drill press or other stationary power tool. These pumps don't make much noise and it's just enough air to keep the dust away from your work but without blowing it all over your shop. Wrap a piece of soft wire around the hose so it can be pointed anywhere you want

Mark Woods
Danville, Illinois

Useful Hole in Sawhorse

A hole drilled in top of a sawhorse serves many purposes. You can drive nails out of used material through it, drill holes in a project, drive dowels into wheels, etc.

John J. Williams
Paulsboro, New Jersey

Double Up for Disk Saving

To get every minute of use out of your sanding disks, glue two 5-inch sanding disks together, back-to-back. The result is a stiffer disk that lasts four to five times longer than a single-ply sanding disk. When one side of the disk gives out, simply turn it over for a fresh sanding surface.

Charles Pulliam
Belleville, Illinois

Conform Leather to Fit Your Tools

An off-the-shelf leather scabbard or tool holder for your tool belt can be custom molded to your tool or knife. Soak the leather in rubbing alcohol. Then wrap the tool in plastic wrap to prevent it from rusting. Insert it in the holder and form the leather around it. The top edge can be rolled slightly to make it easier to insert the tool. When the leather dries, it will fit the tool perfectly. This is useful for forming a belt holder for a power screwdriver or drill.

Hal Handy.

Make Your Own Battery Cable Terminal

A small piece of copper tubing flattened in a vise and drilled to the proper size makes a great temporary battery cable terminal. Just solder the copper piece to your cable.

John J. Williams
Paulsboro, New Jersey

Easy Drill Press Adjustments with Rubber Washer

Install a rubber hose washer between the two adjusting nuts of the depth gauge on your drill press. That way you won't need to use pliers or a wrench when changing the allowable depth.

William K. Vatter
Springfield, Ohio

True Grit

If you find you go through a lot of sandpaper on your orbital sander because of tearing rather than wearing, here's an inexpensive solution. Cover the back of the sandpaper with duct tape before clamping it to your sander. Now you can use the sheets until the grit is fully worn. The tape has the added advantage of stiffening the paper, which in turn transfers more of the sanding power to the workpiece.

Lisa Tiedemann
Schoharie, New York

Save Your Broken Hacksaw Blades

Don't throw away broken hacksaw blades. Hacksaw blades, if still sharp, make great little saws even when you can no longer fit them into a handle. Simply make a handle by wrapping one end of the broken blade with tape. Keep this handy little saw in your tool box for sawing in tight spots.

Handyman Club Staff

Keep Track of 35mm Canister Storage

If you use 35mm film canisters to store small brads, nails, screws or other small parts, try this tip. Drill a ³⁄₁₆" hole in the center of the cap. Thread a nut half way on a ³⁄₁₆" eye bolt that has about 1" of thread. Insert the threaded part of the eye bolt through the hole in the cap until it fits against the nut. Thread a second nut onto the end of the bolt and tighten it against the bottom of the cap. Put the cap back on the 35mm film container. Now you can hang it from a long nail, coffee cup hook, or a long pegboard hook. Fuji Film makes their canisters out of clear plastic, for instant identification. If you use the black containers, be sure to label them.

Steve Simonton
Tampa, Florida

If All Else Fails–Hang On to Those Manuals

Most Handyman Club of America Members have power tools and machines in their home shops. Naturally, each of them comes with a registration card, owner's manual and other material. It always seems that when it's time to do maintenance or a special setup procedure on your tools, the owner's manuals are no where to be found.

Solve that problem by buying a sturdy 3-ring binder and file all of your materials in it. For smaller booklets and manuals, use top-loading vinyl sleeves made for holding papers in 3-ring binders. By doing so, you'll have all of your manuals in one handy place. In case of theft or other loss, the collection of manuals could be helpful in telling police exactly what tools were taken and in proving to an insurance company what tools you owned.

Harry Larks
New Orleans, Louisiana

Prevent Drawers from Pulling Out

One of the most exasperating accidents in the shop is when you open a drawer and it pulls all the way out and spills everything on the floor. A good way to prevent that from happening is to cut a piece of wood about 2" long and screw one end into the back of the drawer near the top. Put the drawer back in the chest and turn the block of wood so that it sticks up higher than the top edge of the drawer. The block of wood will then hit against the cabinet facing when the drawer is pulled open and stop it from moving forward. When you need to remove the drawer from the cabinet, simply reach in and turn the piece of wood down so that the drawer will slide out.

Handyman Club Staff

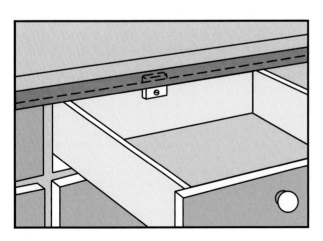

Bonus from Bulk Buying

If you use more than a few utility knife blades each year, buy them in bulk. You can buy 100 utility knife blades in a plastic holder for about $10 instead of nearly $2 for just five of them. This is a savings of 30 cents per blade. Mount the dispenser to a convenient surface and fresh blades will always be at hand.

John J. Williams
Paulsboro, New Jersey

Dispense Small Brads and Screws

Magnetic paper clip dispensers are great for dispensing small steel brads, screws and nuts. Several can be used for dispensing and storing commonly used items, but just one as a dispenser for the fastener of the day saves time and parts.

John J. Williams
Paulsboro, New Jersey

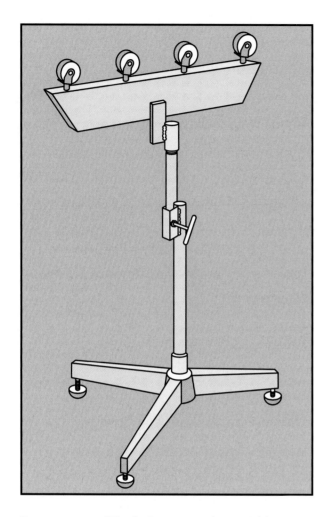

Inexpensive Work Supports from Old Caster Wheels

If you've ever ripped long lumber on a table saw alone, you know how nice it would be for some of those expensive rollers to support your work. You can make an inexpensive set of work supports from old caster wheels mounted on almost any piece of solid wood (see illustration). They will be multi-directional, similar to the expensive roller balls, and you can make them from old office chair bases. You can also make brackets to attach the work supports to sawhorses, making them more portable.

Mark Woods
Danville, Illinois

Fix Loose or Replaced Handles

When you change the wooden handle on an old tool or buy a new tool that has a wooden handle, a little epoxy will make them safer. Set the wedge(s) into the top of the handle and then pour a little 2-part epoxy on the wedge. This will keep the wedge where it supposed to be and you won't have to fight with a sliding, and potentially dangerous, head on your tool anymore.

Stephen Cantelli
Strafford, New Hampshire

Magnetic Strips in the Shop

Magnetic strips can be very useful in your shop or work area. They make excellent holders for screws, nuts, bolts and other small parts. You can buy the style with a white surface that can be written on with a marker and easily erased. Cut them into strips and use them to mark the contents of your workshop drawers. They can also easily be removed or changed as needed.

John J. Williams
Paulsboro, New Jersey

Handy Tool for Connecting Chain

Roller chains, that look like bicycle chains, are used for powering several kinds of lawn and garden equipment, including self-propelled lawnmowers as well as many garage door openers. Trying to re-connect these chains while they're on the sprockets can be tough. If you regularly deal with these chains, make a set of tools for holding the roller chains in place so they can be connected with pins. Grind an appropriate notch, big enough to hold a roller chain axle, in each jaw of a Vise-Grip longnose locking pliers. To use the tool, run the chains over their sprockets and plan to join them where they're away from sprockets, connectors or tensioners. Put the last roller axle from the two end links, one in a notch on each jaw of the pliers, and then squeeze the pliers to bring both ends together. If you work with different sized chain, grind different notches in appropriate size Vise-Grip locking pliers.

Charles Weber
Howard Lake, Minnesota

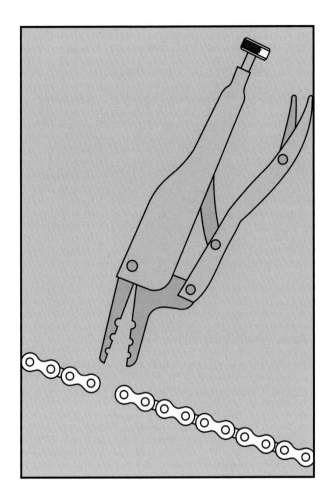

Extend the Life of Your Scroll Saw Blades

Get additional use from your scroll saw blades by clamping a board at least as thick as the length of your scroll saw's stroke to the saw table–usually about ¾". This puts the sawing action on new teeth above the worn out ones.

David Nolt
Versailles, Missouri

Permanent Drill Press Key Solution

Never lose your drill press chuck key again. Use some epoxy to glue a magnet on the front of your drill press then use it to hold the chuck key.

Dennis Respalje
Brandon, Wisconsin

Clamp Down on Power Tool Discharge

If there is a difference between the diameter of the discharge of a power tool and your shop vac's hose, connect the discharge opening to the hose with a rubber connection used for joining large pipes. The connectors come with hose clamps. Attach one end of the connector to the outlet source and the other to the vacuum hose. This doesn't need to be an air-tight seal, so you can clamp the connector by tightening the hose clamp.

David C. Fuller
Elyria, Ohio

Take Shock Protection with You

To reduce the likelihood of a serious shock in the shop work site, a portable ground-fault circuit interrupt is a great investment. It is easily moved from receptacle to receptacle, it provides protection if your shop is located where it can get damp, such as a basement or garage. You may not need a GFCI with double insulated tools, but it can't hurt.

John J. Williams
Paulsboro, New Jersey

Household Saw Blade Cleaner

To clean pitch build-up from saw blades, use Easy-Off oven cleaner. I just follow the instructions on the can for cleaning a cold oven.

Jerry L. Vess
Mt. Eaton, Ohio

Provide Comfortable Protection

Goggles are good at protecting eyes from flying debris. But who wants a pop in the snout, either? Face shields provide more coverage, are usually more comfortable and easily fit over glasses. In addition, like a welder's mask, they flip out of the way when you need a better look.

John J. Williams
Paulsboro, New Jersey

Take the Shock Out of Your Punch

Rubber handles, usually bought for pliers, work well on center punches and nail sets, too. They make your tools easier to grip, more comfortable and they absorb much of the shock when you strike the tool. Slide them over the punch or set and cut off the closed end to expose the head of the tool.

John J. Williams
Paulsboro, New Jersey

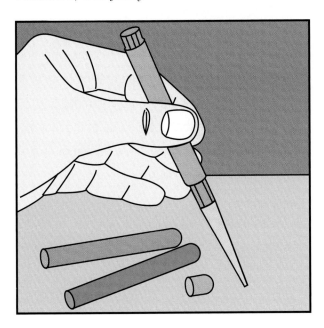

Colored Sticks are Easier to Find

If you have a hard time keeping track of your power tool push sticks among all the scraps and clutter in your shop, here's a solution. Paint the handles of your push sticks so that they stand out from all the other pieces of wood. That may sound like too much work, but it's probably less than making all those new push sticks.

Dennis Respalje
Brandon, Wisconsin

Heavy Duty Homemade Leather Punch

To make a quick and inexpensive hole punch for leather, rubber or other soft material, use a short piece of steel pipe with an inside diameter the size of the desired hole. Grind the outside edge of one end to a sharp taper. This punch will last longer if the non-sharpened edge is threaded and a cap is screwed on for a striking face.

Jerry L. Vess
Mt. Eaton, Ohio

Let Your Wood Boxes Glide Across the Floor

Chair glides, designed to go on the end of a wooden chair leg to prevent the legs from marring a kitchen floor, make excellent feet for any wooden boxes in your shop. If your shop has a vinyl floor, the plastic guides are almost like wheels. The plastic ones will protect a wooden floor best. But if your shop is on concrete, use the metal ones.

John J. Williams
Paulsboro, New Jersey

Right-Angle Plugs for Power Tool Cords

Few things are as frustrating as having a power cord pull out of the extension cord when you're using a power tool. When you knot the two cords together, the knot seems to get caught on everything. The problem can be minimized by replacing the plug on the power tool cord with a right-angle plug. Since the pull on the cord is not in line with the plug and socket, it is much harder to pull the plugs apart accidentally.

Hal Handy

Compartmentalize Your Parts

Keep a small supply of empty egg cartons in your shop. They'll come in handy when you're taking apart something that requires re-assembly in the same order. When you remove parts, lay them one at a time in successive compartments in the egg carton. That way when you're ready for re-assembly, you simply reverse the order and they'll go back on correctly.

Handyman Club Staff

Reduce Moisture from Compressed Air

One of the most important functions of an air compressor is to deliver clean, dry air. One of the easiest ways to lower the moisture content of compressed air is to add 50 feet of hose, which you can leave coiled, or a piping system between a good coalescing filter and the receiver tank. The reason is that the air temperature leaving a compressor can reach up to 300 degrees F.

Air that hot can hold a lot of moisture that will condense quickly inside your tools when the air expands and cools. Moisture can rust the workings of a sander or ratchet. But it can really foul up a finish if you're using a paint gun. When painting, take the 50 ft. hose that is coiled up at the foot of your compressor and place it in a bucket of cold water for even more cooling

David Stecker
St. Louis, Missouri

Practically Priceless Workshop Clamps

If you need lots of little clamps for a project, saw a section of 2 or 3 inch PVC pipe into inch-wide rings. Then saw through the rings. They provide about 8 pounds of pressure when opened an inch. These clamps may not be as convenient as regular spring clamps, but because you get more than 100 of them from a 10-ft section of pipe, you can't beat the price.

Nathan Jagoditsh
Ventura, California

Sawdust-Free Wheelin' on the Band Saw

Here's a way to keep sawdust from fouling the rubber wheels on a band saw. Cut off the end of a toothbrush. Heat it up with a hair dryer and bend the shaft to a right angle. Then mount the brush against the wheel, attaching it with a sheet metal screw or a hose clamp, depending on the saw.

Alvin Sudno
Boothwyn, Pennsylvania

Soften the Blow

Get a rubber crutch tip large enough to go over the striking head of your hammer. It makes a hammer into a mallet. It's great for putting dado joints together, striking wooden-handled tools, working with plastic and soft metal parts that you don't want to damage. For those who are always trying to have dual-purpose tools in their tool belt, the tip is a light weight way to have a mallet.

Daniel McNanus
Oswego, New York

Long Storing PVC Pipes

Scrap lengths of PVC pipe provide excellent storage containers for long slender shop items such as dowels, small trim, molding and tubing. Attach two or three sections of various diameter PVC pipe either vertically on the wall or horizontally along the rafters of your shop. Sliding the items to be stored inside the pipes will keep them organized and safe from accidental breakage.

John J. Williams
Paulsboro, New Jersey

Keep Your Dust Pan and Brush Together

Most shops have a dust pan for collecting sawdust and other waste, and a brush or small broom for sweeping the dust into it. The problem seems to be finding both of them at the same time. Drill a small hole in the handle of the brush and tie a short string through it. Slip the string over the handle of your dust pan and store them together.

John J. Williams
Paulsboro, New Jersey

Install Inaccessible Screws

Sometimes you must put a screw in a place that is not accessible with both hands. If you don't have a screw driver with a magnetic tip, try putting a small dab of automotive grease in the slot of the screw. This usually holds the screw in place until you get it started.

Mike Stockford
Milton-Freewater, Oregon

Drill It On the Level

Some new drills have a built-in level to ensure a proper bit angle. If your drill doesn't, here's an easy and inexpensive way to retrofit it with this feature. Tape a line level to the top of your drill. If it doesn't have a flat top, you may need to shim the level to align it with the bit.

Marion Parcus
Terre Haute, Indiana

Slick Bits Don't Stick

One way to keep router and laminate trimmer bits clean is by coating them with petroleum jelly. The lubrication keeps glue and shavings from building up and causing the blade to wander and overheat.

Jan-Carl Aserlind
Frisco, Colorado

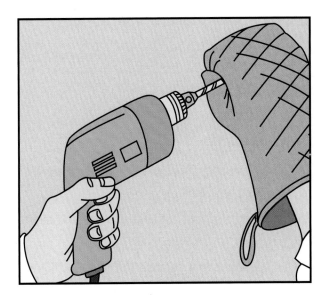

Pot Holders Will Keep Fingers Cool

When removing a bit from your router, use a kitchen pot holder. The pot holder will protect your fingers from being burned by a hot bit or cut by the sharp steel or carbide. It will also protect the bit from damage.

William K. Vatter
Springfield, Ohio

Inexpensive, Disposable Stop Gauges

Small pieces of various tapes, such as masking tape, electrical tape or duct tape, create visible and inexpensive stop gauges on drill bits. You don't have to worry about them hurting the blade or sizes. But don't depend on them to actually stop the drill from cutting past a certain depth.

John J. Williams
Paulsboro, New Jersey

Every Bit Better

You can leave your small drill bits and screwdriver tips hanging around-literally. Install a magnet on the inside lid of a your cordless drill box and stick the bits there. You can paint the tips you use most commonly with bright paint so you'll know which tip to grab in a hurry.

Nathan Anderson
Minneapolis, Minnesota

Wrenches at the Ready

Here's how to make sure the proper wrench is handy when you need to change blades or bits or to adjust a stationary power tool. Use strong magnets, such as those from discarded stereo speakers, to secure wrenches, chuck keys and the like to their respective tools.

William Aubuchon
Barnett, Missouri

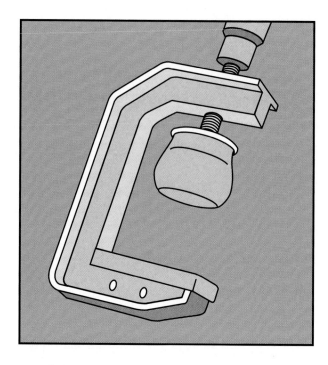

Bottled Water Caps are Tops

Many homes, offices and businesses use bottled water. The caps from these bottles can be very handy around the shop. Use them on the ends of C-clamps to prevent marring the item you're clamping. Place them under machine legs to help keep the vibrations at a minimum. You can use them as plastic fillers or washers in between items as well.

Christopher Klinger
Brewick, Pennsylvania

Keep Your Hand Drill Hanging Around

For those times when you need to drill just one small hole, a hand drill still comes in handy. To make sure the hand drill is always "handy," clamp an eye bolt in the chuck and then hang it on a pegboard hook.

Eugene Westly
Lemon Springs, North Carolina

This Drilling Tip is On the Level

Here's a tip for keeping a drill bit level. Simply slip an oversized washer on the bit before drilling a horizontal hole. If the washer slides toward the tip of the spinning bit, lower the drill. If it slides toward you, raise the drill.

C. U. Gebsen
Bayou LaBatre, Alabama

Screw Gripper

Removing stubborn screws is one of the most maddening tasks. The temptation is to put a lot of torque on the head, but if the bit slips out of the slot it destroys the screw head. That makes it even tougher to remove. Instead, dip the tip of the screwdriver in valve-grinding compound, which can be bought at any auto parts store. The grit in the compound greatly increases the ability of the screwdriver to grip the slot.

Arthur Elson
Troy, Ohio

Chalk One Up for Faster Filing

Soft, non-ferrous metals such as aluminum and brass can clog a file pretty fast and slow your work. You can minimize the problem if you rub the file with chalk first.

Nathan Jagoditsh
Ventura, California

Shop Woodworking

Hacksaw Blades Detail Dovetail

You can use old hacksaw blades to remove waste wood when cutting dovetails. Glue together hacksaw blades (used or broken ones work fine) with the teeth on each blade pointing in the opposite direction of those adjacent to it. Cut the side of the pins and tails to the scribed depth. Remove as much waste as possible using a chisel or a flat-bottomed drill bit. Then use the glued-up blades to remove the remaining waste. The larger the dovetail, the more blades you'll need to glue together. This tool leaves a fine and square cut at the bottoms of the tails and pins.

Henry Ibarra
Corpus Christi, Texas

Remove Paint from Intricate Surfaces

Stripping paint off carved furniture, fancy moldings and picture frames can be done easier with a little sawdust. Flood the area to be stripped with a thin paint stripper, not a gel type. Let it sit for a few minutes, then cover it with about an inch of sawdust. Work the sawdust into all the cracks and crevices with a stiff bristle or brass brush. The sawdust absorbs the paint as it is loosened and helps keep the paint remover from evaporating.If things get too gooey, just add more sawdust.

Hal Handy

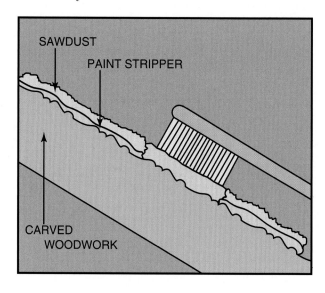

SAWDUST
PAINT STRIPPER
CARVED WOODWORK

Installing Deck Boards

Deck boards that cup up, and thus hold water, will rot faster than those that lay flat or those where the edges turn down. To minimize cupping, whenever possible, install deck boards with the bark side up. The grain pattern on the ends of the boards will tell you which side should be up. The grain should look like a mountain (where water runs from), not a valley (where water runs to).

Hal Handy

Silicone Caulk for Screwing into Hardwood

Silicone caulk is a better lubricant than wax for driving screws into hardwood. An additional benefit is when it sets, it also acts as an adhesive. When you're unable to squeeze anything more out of a tube of caulk with a caulk gun, there is plenty of caulk for a few dozen screws. To make the tube easier to handle, cut off excess cardboard behind the plunger and remove the nozzle at the front of the tube. A piece of duct tape will seal the nozzle end.

Hal Handy

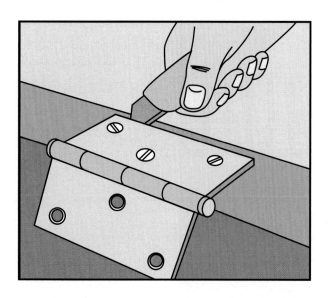

Mortise Butt Hinges

A router template and router are sometimes overkill–or not available–when setting just one or two butt hinges. A quick way to mortise a butt hinge without power tools is to screw the hinge leaf into place. Score around the leaf with a utility knife, making several passes to get the depth of mortise desired. Then remove the leaf and cut out the mortise with a chisel. The hinge can then be reattached, using the same screw holes for alignment.

Hal Handy

Smoother Applications of Stains

Using old rags, instead of brushes, to apply stain is a way to save money and preferred by some. But they can be messy and not as uniform. For less dripping and a smoother application of stains, wrap a small piece of regular household sponge into your staining rag.

Walter Petrowski
Aurora, Colorado

Keep Your Goggles Clean and Soft

It's tough to clean all the dirt and dust off safety goggles. Next time try cleaning them with fabric softener sheets that have been through the dryer once. Fresh ones leave a sticky film. Those that have been through a dryer cycle retain just enough of their anti-static coating to latch onto dust.

Chuck Kubi
Cheyenne, Wyoming

A Simple Jig for Straight Holes

Often a project will call for you to drill a hole and keep it perpendicular to the work surface. Fasten two blocks of wood at a 90° angle and use the joint of the two blocks as a guide to drill a straight hole. Position your drill bit in the corner of the two blocks of wood and the hole will be correct.

Handyman Club Staff

Gluing a Mitered Box

Gluing a mitered box can be a nightmare because the parts keep slipping around. This frustration can be minimized with good old-fashioned masking tape. First, stretch masking tape with the sticky side up across your workbench and put the mitered pieces on the tape end-to-end with the miters touching. Next, simply fold the miters closed so the pieces form a box. Then clamp the box with a bond clamp. The tape will keep the miters from sliding around.

Robert Birkholz
Sun Lakes, Arizona

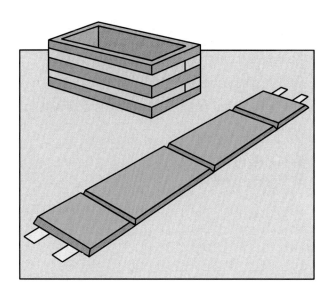

Handy Stain Applicator

Inexpensive squirt bottles with an adjustable nozzle can save many hours when it comes to getting stain or tung-oil like products onto a project in a hurry. Using these bottles speeds up the operation and allows for keeping the surface damp as required for most hand-rubbed oils. They also make it easy to get into tight spots.

Bart Taylor
Tuolumne, California

Getting an Edge on Straight Plywood

When using a circular saw to make long cuts from a sheet of plywood, it can be difficult to get a smooth edge. For long, perfectly straight cuts, use a straight metal bar to guide the saw. First, pencil the cutting line on the material. Then clamp the guide bar to your sheet of plywood so that the left edge of the saw rests against the bar with the blade at the cut point. With the waste to the right, and the left side of the saw's base against the bar, make the cut. Sliding the saw against the bar keeps the saw precisely on the cut-line. This procedure gives a table-saw quality cut with a circular saw.

If you're making many long cuts on plywood, you can make them even quicker by using spacers that are the exact length of the distance between the blade and left edge of the base on your saw. As you normally would, draw the cut line and then place one end of the spacers on the line and the other against the bar. Then clamp the bar and make your cut.

To avoid pencil marks on your finished piece, simply make a tick mark at each end of your piece and align the spacers on those tick marks. This will save you from having to sand the marks off after you're finished.

Glenn N. Willis, Jr.
Redondo Beach, California

Bubbles Forming in Polyurethane

If bubbles form when applying polyurethane varnish, simply blow on them gently. For larger jobs, a small fan or a hairdryer on the cool setting works great.

Walter Petrowski
Aurora, Colorado

Judge the Depth While Drilling Holes

Here's a way to easily judge the depth when drilling holes in wood projects. It's especially helpful when you don't want to drill through the material on which you're working. Take a white or other brightly colored twist tie, such as those used for trash bags, and wrap it around the drill bit at the desired depth. It's easy to see and if twisted snugly won't ride up or down the bit.

Michael Walston
Jacksonville, Florida

Remove Finish from Turned Legs

To remove old finish from curved or turned table legs, place paper or a drop cloth under the leg and apply finish remover with a brush, then use twisted burlap to get into the grooves. Use twine or coarse string to get into narrow openings. Before applying new stain, go over the surface with lacquer thinner to neutralize the effects of the remover.

Kenneth Haner
Covina, California

Gluing Curved Laminated Forms

Curves on furniture, handrails and trim are just a few of the reasons for forming layers of thin laminations of wood into a final part. Thin strips of wood, like the layers of plywood, are bent to a form, clamped and glued. However, when the final product is removed from the form, there is a tendency for the piece to spring back with time. Drilling and pounding hardwood dowels, liberally coated with glue, through the laminated section will reduce the springback considerably. The outer lamination can be left off until the core and dowels have dried. Then the final layer is glued on to cover the ends of the dowels. Nails or screws would work, but by using dowels you won't hit any metal with other woodworking tools when assembling the finished product.

Hal Handy

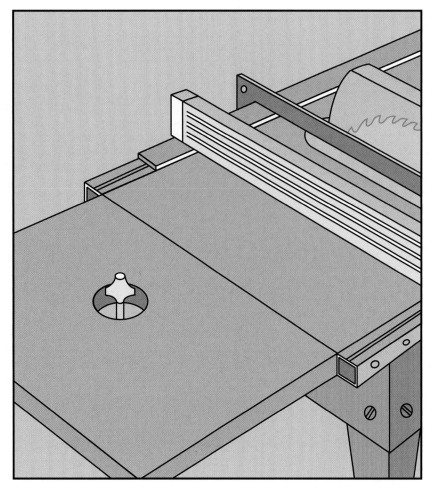

Cleaning Sandpaper

Cleaning clogged sandpaper is an excellent way to save money in the workshop. For rotating belts, drums and discs, crepe rubber blocks do a good job of unclogging the abrasive. However, for vibrating sanders and sanding blocks, a small brass-bristled brush, the kind used to renew the surface of suede shoes, does a good job of removing wood dust.

Hilbert Teske
Winfield, Illinois

Out of the Kitchen and Into the Shop

An old kitchen table with a Formica top works great as a table saw extension and router table. Cut the table to fit on the back end of your saw. Use saw horse legs to get it to the right height. Be sure to leave room for a rip fence to move back and forth on the saw.

You can also cut a 2" hole in an end of the old table and counter sink three screw holes to mount your router underneath. This makes for a larger and smoother router table.

Dave Lee
Dakota City, Iowa

Saddle Blankets for a Sawhorse

If your work has ever suffered when a protective pad slid off a sawhorse, leaving scratches in your project, try this method. Slit a length of foam insulation tube intended for ¾-inch pipes on your sawhorses. The foam grips the sawhorse top lightly enough to stay in place when needed, and the tubes can be quickly removed on jobs where padding is not required.

Paul Houle
North Smithfield, Rhode Island

Store Sandpaper

Storing sandpaper can be a frustrating problem because it can become folded and torn. Use a six-pocket, letter-size file folder to hold up to 9"x12" inch sheets of sandpaper. Put a different grade of sandpaper in each of the pockets. The folder will keep the sandpaper flat and organized so you'll know how much of each grade you have when planning a project. Folders with more pockets are available if you need to store more than six grades of paper.

Hilbert Teske
Winfield, Illinois

Route a Prefect Circle

It's very difficult to rout a perfect circle in a board free-hand. If you'll outline the hole first with a circle cutter to the bottom depth, you can route with a straight bit. Take several passes with the router. The cutter and bit must be set to cut equal depth for a flat bottom. If the depression is for a flower pot, set the bit to go completely through the board for a drain hole.

Charles O. Bender
Jacksonville, Florida

Construct Toy Train Wheels Fast and Easy

Almost everybody loves toy trains–especially kids. For many people making the wheels can take too much time and effort. But you can construct train wheels in no time with a circle cutter. Cut about two-thirds of the way through a piece of ½" thick solid stock. Then flip over the work piece and extend the cutter arm by the width of the cutter then complete the cut from the opposite face. To cut several wheels to uniform dimensions, set the depth stop on the drill press for the first cut.

Handyman Club Staff

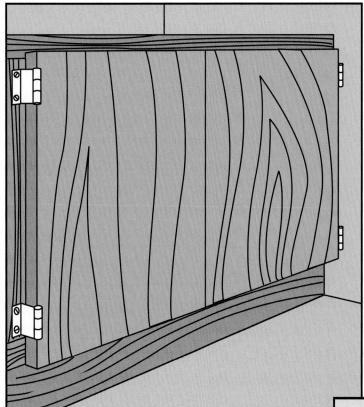

Fine Finish with Steel Wool

After applying the final finishing coat to a piece of furniture, use paste furniture polish on fine steel wool to remove trapped dust and other minor rough spots. This gives you a smooth finish and leaves no scratches.

Howard W. Leonard
Oak Bluffs, Massachusetts

Mount Two Cabinet Doors without Stile

When building a cabinet for a double-wide sink base or bathroom vanity, you usually will need two doors. Normally, the opening will have no center stile to provide better access for faucets, drain lines and storage. It can be difficult to align these doors with a good center gap. An easy way to accomplish this is to cut the door material as if it were a one piece door. After adjusting the fit, mount this one door with four hinges–two at each side. Then, remove the door and rip it at the exact center with a plywood or hollow-ground planer saw blade. When you remount the doors using the same screw holes, you now have a perfect center gap and doors that are aligned perfectly, top and bottom.

Ron Leeman
Casco, Maine

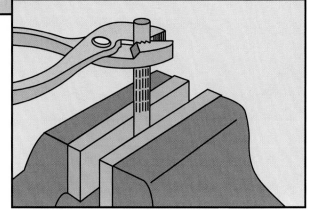

Fluted Dowels

If you don't have fluted dowels or a die to make them, you can make them with one of the most common workshop tools. Crimp the dowel with the large teeth of an ordinary slip-joint pliers. Crimp them so the tooth marks run down the length of the dowel and then rotate the dowel to the next side and repeat.

D.E. Sellars
Ventress, Louisiana

Polish Table and Fence for Ease of Movement

To slide wood and jigs across the table and along the fence of your table saw or router table with minimum effort, polish the surface with steel wool. Then clean the area with mineral spirits. When it's dry, wax it with car wax.

David Stecker
St. Louis, Missouri

Put the Squeeze On Broken Furniture Legs

The conventional way of fixing a broken round furniture leg often seems like more trouble than the broken leg itself. The old way is to build a jig to hold the leg, then glue the leg and clamp it in the jig with a C-clamp. A faster way to do it is to use a stainless steel hose clamp to go around the leg. They are sold in a variety of sizes, up to 4 inches at auto parts stores. To avoid marring the leg when tightening the clamp, insert a strip of cardboard between the hose clamp and the leg.

Handyman Club Staff

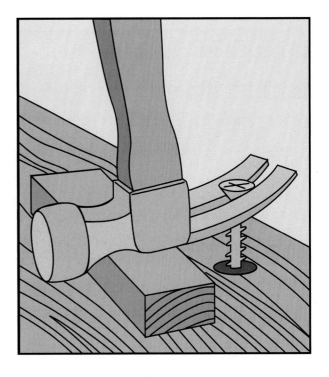

Remove Old Dowels

It seems as if one chair or another is always in need of repair. Many chairs are assembled with dowels and removing the old dowels is difficult. If it's a ⅜" dowel and you try to drill it out with a ⅜" bit, the dowel is usually harder than the surrounding wood and the bit will wander off center. That causes a sloppy, virtually useless hole for the new dowel.

First, pull out the broken dowel ends using the following procedure. Drill a pilot hole and screw a 1¼" drywall screw into the center of the old dowel. Use a claw hammer and try to pull the old dowel. Use shims under the hammer head to keep the force going straight out and to avoid marring the wood surface. If the screw pulls out without the dowel, drill into the dowel with a bit slightly smaller than the original dowel size. Then use a small chisel to clean out the hole.

Joseph A. Schumacher
St. Paul, Minnesota

101

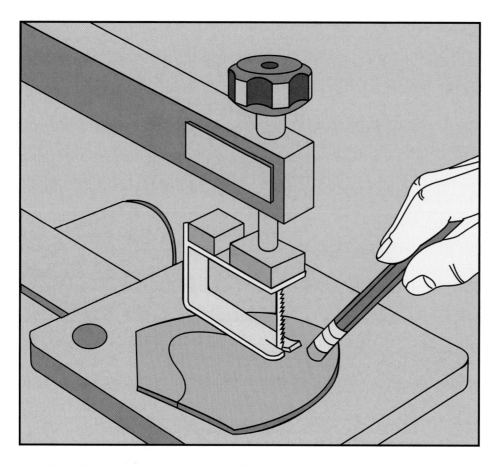

Cut Small Wood Pieces on a Scroll Saw

When cutting small pieces with a scroll saw, the
eraser end of a pencil is a very helpful "push stick."
It steadies the wood and keeps my fingers out of
the way.

Dennis Respalje
Brandon, Wisconsin

Tie One On

When using a web clamp to hold projects such
as an oval picture frame, tie several strings through
the frame and around the web to hold it in place.
This will keep the web from falling off while you
cinch it up.

George Cole
Sequim, Washington

Post Those Measurements

Although Post-it Notes™ are designed for
the office, they're the best way to keep track of
measurements in the shop, too. They allow you to
make several measurements at once on different
pages and then each page can be stuck on the
actual pieces with which you're working. They
leave no residue and won't harm finishes. Best
of all, they're small enough to fit into a pocket
or tool belt.

Jeremy Powers
Fridley, Minnesota

Best Way to Cut Plywood Splinter Free

Want to get the smoothest edge when cross cutting a piece of plywood? First, determine where the cut is to be made and cut the surface of the plywood with a sharp utility knife. Then, using that score mark, set up a straight edge on which to run the foot of your saw. Finally, take a piece of good 3" masking tape and cover the area to be cut.

The saw blade should be sharp, but it's more important that it be clean. Wood fibers are tugged up by the pitch as much as by the blade's teeth. Clean the blade with mineral spirits and a wire brush. After making the cut, remove the masking tape by pulling it the short way to the edge, not the long way across the grain.

Jeremy Powers
Fridley, Minnesota

Clamp Small Items

Keep a supply of rubber bands and snap-type clothes pins in your shop. Together, they make great little clamps for small items.

John J. Williams
Paulsboro, New Jersey

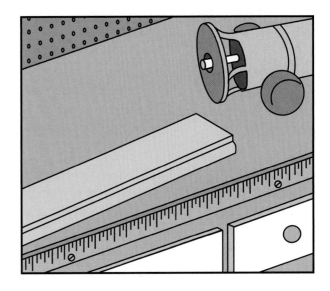

Handy "No Hands" Measurement

A yardstick attached to the front edge of your workbench provides quick "no hands" measurements.

John J. Williams
Paulsboro, New Jersey

Keep Nail and Screw Lubricant Handy

Just like screws, lubricated nails are less likely to split wood. Coat the pointed end of a nail with beeswax or paraffin before nailing. Keep the lubricant handy by storing it in a ½" diameter x ¾" deep hole drilled in the hammer handle. Melt beeswax or paraffin on a stove, then pour it into the hole. If the wax you're using is soft enough, use a spackling knife and force it into the hole.

Handyman Club Staff

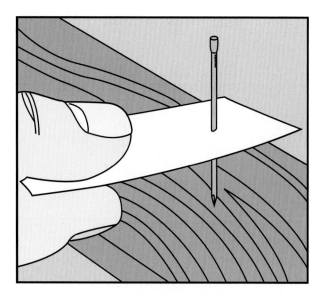

Handy Finger Saver Idea

A two-inch strip of plastic, cut from the lid of a margarine tub, and with a small hole punched in it, provides a good support for hammering small brads. The brad, which is difficult to hold, can be pushed through the hole. The strip is then lifted off when the brad is started. You'll also keep your fingers out of the hammer strike zone.

John J. Williams
Paulsboro, New Jersey

An Added Measure

Add an 18" extender board to the miter gauge of a table saw, at a 90-degree angle to the blade. Then measuring from the blade, carefully mark off inches on the stick. You can now cut short board lengths by lining the edge of the board to be cut to the appropriate inch mark on the gauge.

George Cole
Sequim, Washington

Two Ways to Measure Diameters

Without a pair of calipers, accurately measuring the diameter of any object smaller than 1 inch can be difficult. It's also tough to determine the exact diameter of large round objects.

For smaller items, use two squarely cut wood strips and a ruler. Butt the two strips against the item you're measuring, such as a bolt or toy part, as you would the jaws of a caliper. Then measure the distance between them. On larger items, use two framing squares on a level surface, such as a board or the floor. Hold the squares up to the side of the object and measure the distance on the level surface.

Handyman Club Staff

Sewing Needle Makes Good Tiny Drill Bit

Occasionally a project calls for a tiny hole. Most workshops don't have bits smaller than $\frac{1}{16}$." To bore a tiny hole use a sewing machine needle in your drill. Sewing machine needles come in different sizes and styles at fabric stores and sewing machine dealers. Choose needles with sharp points instead of blunt-end styles. Also look for an enlarged shank to give your chuck a good grip on the needle. Drill at slow speeds to avoid burning.

Handyman Club Staff

Coating Screws with Wax

To lubricate screw threads for easier driving, push the screws into a wax toilet seal before using them. The soft wax will adhere to the screws better than wax from an old candle. These toilet seals cost just a couple of dollars at home centers. If you place the round seal on an 8" square of plywood, you'll also have a convenient way to carry the screws. A variety of the screws can be stuck in the ring, like an old-fashioned pin cushion, will be ready to use and won't roll away.

John J. Williams
Paulsboro, New Jersey

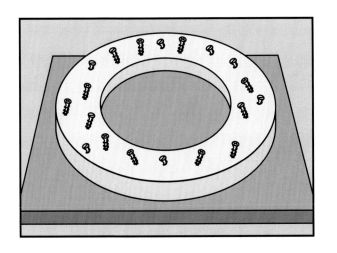

Backing Up Plain Sandpaper

When sanding contours with sandpaper by hand attach duct tape to the back of the sand paper. This makes the sandpaper stronger and more durable.

Steve Forrester
Glade Spring, Virginia

Fill in Holes

Adding dry spackling to premixed putty will help remove any excess oils in the putty.

Greg Stultz
Chicago, Illinois

Plastic Knives Won't Darken Wood Fillers

Plastic food knives make ideal spreaders for many glue jobs. They're disposable, bigger than toothpicks and have a more consistent edge than scraps of wood. When mixing glue with fine sawdust for wood fillers, the mixture won't darken as it would with a metal mixing tool.

George Cole
Sequim, Washington

Safe Way to Rout Little Pieces

Here's a safety tip for routing small pieces. Rout the edges or design on a longer board and then cut the smaller routed piece from larger board.

Gary Moore
Tigard, Oregon

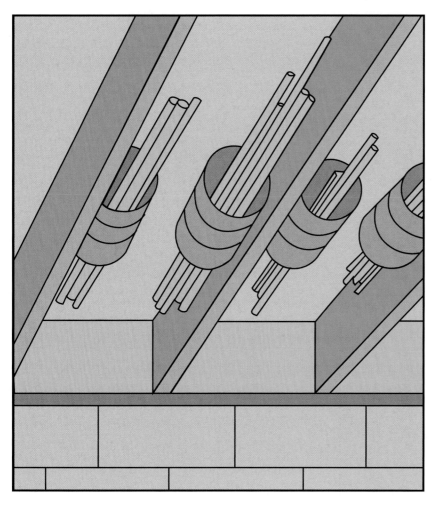

Gap-Proof Joints Between Boards

When screwing together two pieces of wood, a gap sometimes develops between the pieces. The problem is that the screw, as it's driven, dislodges wood fibers on each piece, and these raised fibers form a hump. Slightly countersink the pilot holes on the mating surfaces to prevent a hump from forming. This method ensures gap-free joints every time.

Nancy Silvens
Poughkeepsie, New York

Dowels and Moldings are In the Can

Save coffee cans and other cylindrical containers such as oatmeal cartons. Remove the bottoms and fasten several about a foot apart to the overhead joists in your shop. They make great storage for elongated stock such as dowels, moldings, tubing, etc.

Robert Guyre
Maywood, New Jersey

Get a Final Finish Preview

When final sanding a wood surface, wipe it down with lacquer thinner as part of the final visual inspection before applying a finish. When wet with lacquer thinner, a board shows any cross-grain scratches or dings. Lacquer thinner dries quickly and won't raise the grain. And for oily woods like teak, lacquer thinner will remove the natural oil residue that can retard the varnish's drying time.

Kevin Strecker
Arkansas City, Kansas

Scroll Saw Can Double as Sander

A table top scroll saw and some dull scroll saw blades can double as a light-duty sander. Here's what you need: one or more scroll saw blades (dull ones are fine), yellow woodworker's glue, a 3"x1" wood block and self-adhesive sandpaper. Cut a thin slot lengthwise in the center of the block of wood, about ½" deep. Slip the old blade into the slot, leaving about 1" of exposed blade at each end. Neatly and completely fill the slot with glue. The old blade will then serve as the up and down spindle for the block.

Cut four strips of sandpaper into 1"x3" strips and attach one to each side of the block. Mount the block in your saw using the blade you've glued into it. Turning the saw on will provide a fast up and down action on the block. First, use the front and left side of the block for sanding. When the sandpaper wears out, turn the block upside down remount in the saw and use the other two sides. Let the sandpaper do the work, putting too much pressure on the block could snap the blade or overload the motor.

Eugene Tinnell
Hermitage, Missouri

Used Sanding Belts Still Useful

Used sanding belts from a belt sander or floor finisher, cut to fit various sized wood blocks, make great sanding blocks. Glue to a useful sized block and then wrap it with rubber bands until glue dries. Blocks of various sizes and lengths can be made this way.

George Cole
Sequim, Washington

Set Calipers Quickly with this Gauge

Resetting calipers can quickly become a chore requiring time and increasing the possibility of incorrect settings. Make a gauge to help set the calipers.

Cut a piece of stock that tapers from ½" to 3½" wide. Mark lines at common widths and any specialty widths you use and label them. When you want the caliper set for a specific width, just bring the two ends of the calipers to that mark.

Handyman Club Staff

107

Convertible Web Clamp

Web clamps are handy for clamping together irregularly shaped items and are particularly good at clamping together the legs of a chair. You can make a temporary web clamp by using an old belt (or two) and a Quick-Grip bar clamp. The Quick-Grip uses a pistol action to tighten the clamp. Unlike bar clamps where the clamping pressure is applied with a screw, a Quick-Grip can quickly travel the whole length of the bar. Take an old leather belt and put the belt buckle over one end of a Quick-Grip. Use a Pop Rivet or a small bolt through two of the holes that were used to buckle the belt and put that loop over the other end. Then squeeze the Quick-Grip until it tightens the belt around your work. If you need a longer web, add another belt.

Jeremy Powers
Fridley, Minnesota

Use Smaller, Cheaper Blades to Cut Particle Board

Particle board is hard on saw blades–even carbide tipped blades. When cutting particle board on a table saw, use a cheaper 7¼" carbide tipped blade from a circular saw instead of the expensive 9-inch, 10-inch or 12-inch blades that are made for table saws. Because particle board isn't usually thicker than ¾" the extra cutting depth afforded by a bigger blade isn't needed.

Jeremy Powers
Fridley, Minnesota

Apply Patterns to Wood

When applying a pattern to wood for scroll sawing, put a piece of Con-Tact self-adhesive vinyl on the wood first. Then spray on the adhesive and put the pattern on the Con-Tact paper. If you can, create your pattern on the self-adhesive paper first. This eliminates any other adhesives. Using self-adhesive paper makes removing the pattern a lot easier and reduces the time and effort needed to remove the spray adhesive.

Forrest Bennett
Columbus, Ohio

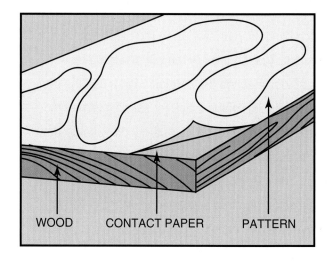

WOOD   CONTACT PAPER   PATTERN

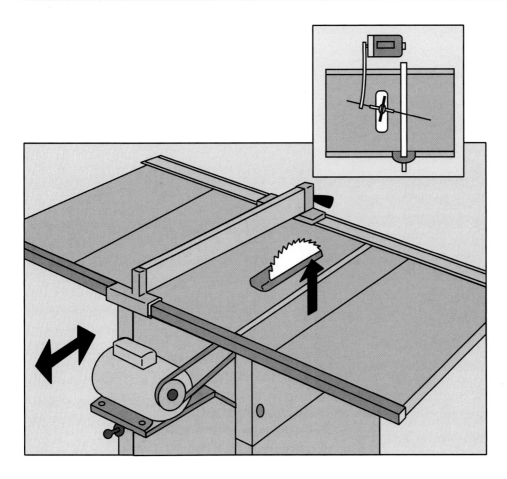

Check Your Belt Tension on Table Saws

Whenever the height of a blade is changed on a belt-drive table saw, it is advisable to check the tension on the belt. On some saws, raising the blade tends to tighten the belt. This may place a radial force on the arbor pulley and cause the blade to be slightly out of line with the rip fence and miter gauge.

Hilbert Teske
Winfield, Illinois

Buckle-Free Board Press

Boards tend to buckle when clamped edge to edge with pipe clamps during gluing because the clamps' screws are above the center of the board and the jaws tend to slant. You can overcome this problem by slipping a wooden dowel, about the same thickness as the boards, in between the end board and the jaws of the clamps. This transfers the pressure to the center of the boards.

Ronald Leeman
Casco, Maine

A Trip to the Art Store Makes Changing Dimensions Easy

Every now and again the home handyman wants to change the size of a project. This often can lead to cumbersome arithmetic. As an example, lets say you want to enlarge a piece of wood that's ⅜" wide and 6" long to 8" long. How wide should it be? A trip to an art supply store can make this an easier chore. A graphic artist's proportional scale (sometimes called an enlargement wheel) makes these kinds of mathematical calculations simple. Just set the original dimension on the rotating scale to the new known measurement. Then, each new dimension will be indicated next to the corresponding original. You can set the wheel to a specific percentage of enlargement or reduction, too, to determine new measurements. They usually cost less than $10.00.

Handyman Club Staff

Scrollsawing Small Letters

When scrollsawing letters that are at least 1 inch high, templates and stencils work fine. But if you want letters smaller, it can be difficult to follow the lines with your blade. Here's a great solution:

For smaller letters and characters, use transfer sheets and rub the letters right onto the wood. You can find them at just about any office supply store in a huge variety of sizes and styles. And you'll have very little trouble following the dark outlines with your saw. When you've finished, the letters will rub off with a pen-knife blade or can be easily sanded away.

Handyman Club Staff

Drill Spheres Safely and Accurately

It's tough drilling holes in wooden balls. It's hard to get a good grip on them with a drill press vise or clamp. To simplify the job make a set of auxiliary jaws that will give a vise or handscrew clamp a firmer hold on all spheres. Cut two pieces of ⅜" thick pine board to fit your clamp or vise jaws (2" by 4" is often a good size). Next drill a ⅜" hole through the center of each. Sandwich the ball to be drilled between the holes, and place the assembly in the vise or clamp for a solid grip. If you have several balls to bore, fasten the auxiliary jaws to the vise with two sided tape.

Handyman Club Staff

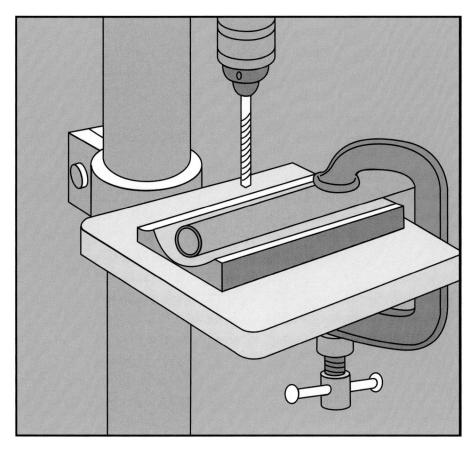

Extra Support for Cylindrical Projects

Pieces of concave crown molding, such as a small cove molding, provide a great support for drilling or working on cylindrical objects. One piece, fastened to a board can be a stop for various sizes of pipe or dowel.

John J. Williams
Paulsboro, New Jersey

Raise High the Pipe Clamps Carpenter

Pipe clamps work well for edge gluing cutting boards, chess boards, tabletops, or similar projects, but it can be frustrating if they roll on their sides as you work. To make the job easier, assemble two pairs of pipe clamp holders from ¾" pipe fittings. Set four ¾"x6"x6" galvanized bases with flanges on the work bench. Insert 6" nipples into these. For each base, cut a T-joint in half so that it splits the piping parts as you would slice a banana for a banana split. In the T-section, just below the straight part, drill a hole through both halves. Tap one side for a 4" thumb screw. The thumb screw will then draw the two parts together like the jaws of a vice. Use these mini vices to clamp the pipes of the pipe clamps and the threads of the 6" nipples. This will hold the clamps about 12" off the bench. Cover the pipe clamp pipes with a single strip of 2" masking tape to protect them from glue drips.

Handyman Club Staff

111

Shop Miscellaneous

Keep Stencils Flat While Spraying

To keep stencils flat while spraying, coat the back surface with a glue stick and lightly attach the stencil to the work. It works great and is easily cleaned off with water. A light coating of an aerosol art adhesive, called spray mount, is handy if the stencils are too small for the broad glue stick or are so big it would use up too many of the sticks.

John J. Williams
Paulsboro, New Jersey

Lubricate Rubber Seals with Soap

When installing rubber O-rings, lip seals and other rubber items that fit tightly, the common practice is to use grease or oil to ease installation. While this will work, petroleum products will deteriorate some forms of rubber. Instead, use common household liquid dish soap. It makes the rubber slide very easily, will not attack the rubber and helps to hold things in place when dry.

Jerry Hogan
Cincinnati, Ohio

A Well Placed Reminder is Half Done

The problem with the traditional "job jar" is it's rarely handy. A small bulletin board mounted near your shop exit is great for posting reminders to pick up drill bits or change the oil in the car. You'll be more likely to get all the parts assembled before starting your next project.

John J. Williams
Paulsboro, New Jersey

Find Small Parts — Time Saver

Many people separate and store small parts in cans with plastic lids, such as coffee cans, powdered milk cans, peanut cans, etc. Each can holds one type of part, such as bolts, nails, screws, washers, etc. When you need a particular size or style of screw, for example, you'll often find yourself dumping the contents of one or more of these cans on to the workbench to find the one you want. Then it's difficult to put the remaining pieces back into the can.

To save time, keep an inexpensive oil-changing pan under your workbench–the kind with a good pour spout for discarding used motor oil. When you need a part, dump the contents of the can into the oil pan, find your part, then pour everything right back into the parts can.

Handyman Club Staff

It's the Better Picker-Upper

A large magnet is handy in and around the home. In the shop, a quick pass of the magnet over a dust pile picks up nails, screws and metal filings for reuse or recycling. In the yard, it picks up stray nails after an outdoor project. If you put a piece of sturdy sheet metal between the parts and the magnet, you can release the debris by separating the sheet metal from the magnet.

Wesley Chong
San Diego, California

The Magnet Idea Is Perfectly Clear

Or, instead of a piece of sheet metal, before using the magnet, place it in a plastic bag. You can still pick up the nails, screws and metal shavings. Then simply turn the bag inside out and pull it off the magnet and the collected debris will be neatly gathered inside the bag.

John Gallagher
Terre Haute, Indiana

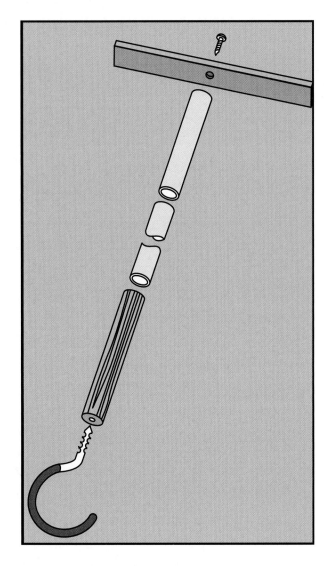

Fetch Stick for Pick-ups

Trucks with a camper shell can be difficult to load and unload, especially if you need to move things in and out of the bed at the front end. To get at things and get them out of the truck with less wear and tear on your back and knees, build a simple device that can be used to lift and pull things such as tool belts, saws, buckets, etc. This device can be left in the truck bed when not in use.

Take a piece of plastic conduit, about 6½ feet long. Glue 1-foot long dowel plugs in each end. On one end, screw in a large hook. On the other, fasten a

4" to 6" long flat piece of metal or wood at a right angle. Plastic conduit is much lighter than a solid pole.

This handy device will make loading and unloading items much easier and will save you a lot of climbing in and out of your truck.

Ross C. Lovington
Sausalito, California

Quickly Drilling Through Furring Strips

Sometimes the home handyman needs to attach a thin furring strip or wooden wedge permanently in place. Using a hammer and nail often is not practical because of a tight location or other obstacles in the way.

A simple solution is to drive a drywall screw through the furring strip or wedge with a power drill or driver. As anyone who has done this knows, this can often split these thin pieces of wood unless a pilot hole is drilled into the wood first. Position the screw and driver at proper location and flip the forward/reverse switch to reverse and "worry" the screw into the wood; it will create a pilot hole without splitting the surface. After the pilot hole has been established, place the drill/driver in forward and turn the screw into place.

Glenn N. Willis
Redondo Beach, California

How to Cool Eager Epoxy

Sometimes two-part epoxy begins to set up before you're through using it. This happens most frequently when you're working in a warm place or during hot weather, because heat speeds up the curing process. To extend the set-up time for epoxy, keep it cool. One way to do this is to mix the ingredients in the recess in the bottom of a cold soft drink can. To do this, just take a full can of a cold soft drink and turn it over. When you're finished gluing, open the pop and pour it over ice to enjoy it without any epoxy mess or fumes.

Handyman Club Staff

Simple Bed Liner for Your Pick-Up

Before loading dirt, gravel, branches, or any other messy load in your pickup, line the bed with one of those cheap plastic tarps. These reinforced tarps are cheap enough that you can get one big enough to even cover the tailgate when it's down. When you are through with the haul, take the plastic tarp out of the truck and shake it–no more sweeping things out of the corners of the bed. If the material you're hauling is light enough, such as landscape bark, the tarp can be used to pull the load out of the truck.

Hal Handy

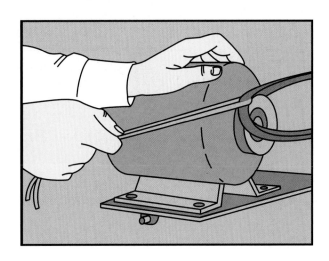

Install Fan Belts Easier

When installing a fan belt or any belt on a pulley, here's a way to make the job easier. Take a piece of cord (thickness of clothesline) and loop it through the belt. Use it to help pull the belt onto the pulley. Rotating the pulley after the belt is on will free the cord. This is very helpful in hard to reach places.

Howard W. Leonard
Oak Bluffs, Massachusetts

115

Emergency Radiator and Heater Hose Repair

For emergency automobile heater and radiator repair patches, carry 3" long pieces of copper pipe in ½" and 1¼" diameters and four hose clamps sized to go around your heater and radiator hoses. At the leak site, cut the hose all the way through. Slip on two clamps and insert the appropriate size copper pipe. Clamp in place and add coolant as needed.

Charles Parker
Aurora, Colorado

First Aid for Smashed Fingers

We know real handymen never hit their fingers with hammers, but should it happen to someone else, here's a tip that may prevent the injured party from losing a fingernail. Grab the smashed finger and apply steady pressure for five minutes. This minimizes internal bleeding and swelling, which can cause the fingernail root to dislodge. Apply ice afterward.

Lucille Arden, Registered Nurse
Austin, Texas

REFERENCE

- Planning and Projects
- Electrical
- Measurements & Conversions
- Nails, Screws and Bolts
- Common Woods, Sizing & Cuts

Reference Contents

Project Guide & Checklist

When working on home improvement projects, there is usually a logical order in which to do the jobs so that they are done in the right order. This reduces the likelihood that one task will have to be undone because the series of tasks were done out of order. Below is a list of jobs in the order they should be done. Not every project will include every item, but find the tasks you need and do them in the order outlined. No order is absolute. If logic dictates a slight shuffle, that's okay. Please make a copy of this and the following pages for every project you work on so you can check off the items as you go.

○ Decide on type of project

○ Measure the room dimensions

○ Inspect concrete supporting walls for cracks

○ Inspect existing framing lumber for soundness and alignment

○ Layout plans to scale

○ Make copies of the plan

○ Submit plans to building inspector

○ Submit plans for bids and estimates

○ Make a list of supplies and tools needed

○ Choose suppliers and contractors

○ Patch and repair concrete walls and floors

○ Frame walls

○ Frame rafters

○ Install roof deck

○ Install exterior sheathing

○ Tie in roofing material with existing roof, shingle

○ Install exterior doors and windows

○ Install soffits and fascia

○ Install siding

○ Caulk exterior joints

○ Rough-in plumbing

○ Rough-in heating

○ Rough-in electrical

○ Rough-in phones and cable TV

○ Install fireplace

○ Call for first inspection

○ Insulate walls

○ Install vapor barrier

○ Insulate or caulk any remaining openings and holes

○ Install bath tub or shower if it has a flange that goes behind the drywall

○ Install drywall, including closets

○ Install ceiling insulation and attic ventilation channels

○ Tape and finish drywall

○ Prime drywall, including ceilings (If ceilings are to be painted, prime again after texturing.)

○ Texture ceilings

○ Install paneling

○ Install cabinets, countertops and vanities

○ Install wood flooring

○ Install interior doors

○ Install moldings and trim

○ Install ceramic tile on floors or walls

○ Paint, stain and varnish

○ Install electric appliances

○ Install remaining plumbing fixtures

○ Install lighting fixtures

○ Install wallcovering

○ Finish electrical, phone and cable

○ Install carpeting and vinyl flooring

○ Call for final inspection

Job Schedule

Project	Materials Bought	Date Begun	Date finished	Inspected
Planning				
Framing				
Roofing				
Exterior siding				
Rough-in plumbing				
Rough-in heating				
Rough-in electrical				
Insulate				
Install drywall				
Finish and prime drywall				
Install cabinets				
Install trim				
Paint				
Set plumbing fixtures				
Hang lighting				
Install wallcovering				
Finish electrical				
Install floor covering				

Drywall

The following is a list of things to look for when installing or inspecting a contractor's job of installing drywall.

○ First, inspect that all electrical, plumbing and framing are in place properly. Make sure electrical boxes are set for the correct drywall thickness. Check the insulation and vapor barrier. Make sure all little holes to the outside are filled with insulation or caulk. Make sure there is backing material to attach drywall to on both sides of all inside (concave) and outside (convex) corners.

○ Insist on or perform the best installation methods. Drywall is no place to get cheap. Use ⅝" drywall. All drywall should be installed perpendicular to framing on both ceilings and walls. Start on the ceilings. Use only coarse-threaded drywall screws measuring 1" to 1½" and use 1¼" ring-shank nails only in places you can't get the screw gun. Countersink all screws and nails, but don't break the surface of the drywall. Bulk drywall is cheap. Don't patch together pieces to save money. You want as few, factory-edged joints to finish as possible. Use drywall or construction adhesive wherever there isn't a vapor barrier, such as inside walls.

○ In bath or kitchen areas, use cementious wallboard, such as USG's Durock, wherever ceramic tile will be installed.

○ Regular drywall offers a good level of fire protection. To increase fire protection near stoves, furnaces and water heaters, a double layer of ⅝" drywall will more than double the protection. For maximum protection, cementious board, such as USG's Durock, is virtually fireproof.

○ On bathroom walls that won't have ceramic tile, use water resistant drywall. Use regular drywall on bathroom ceilings because the water resistant kind can sag. Do not put a vapor barrier behind water resistant drywall. It can trap moisture and is expressly prohibited by drywall makers.

○ On all outside corners, use a nail-on metal bead. The plastic and glue-on corner beads are easy, but if they are hit they will fall apart. All joints should be taped with adhesive fiberglass mesh tape.

○ All joints, outside corners, nails and screws should be covered with three coats of taping compound applied with progressively wider taping knives. Two coats is allowable on inside corners, if the corners are square with two coats. Inside corners must be square for the proper installation of trim. Watch for inside corners that are loaded up with excess compound.

○ At night, with a strong bare-bulb light, look across all walls and ceilings for hollow screw heads and joints and any other rough areas. Also look for hills of taping compound. Mark all spots with a pencil. (Pens can bleed through later.) All joints and surfaces must be perfect. Paint–even textured paint–will accentuate any flaws and make them more noticeable, not less noticeable.

○ Prime all the drywall. Spray textured ceilings after priming the ceiling drywall and again if the ceiling will be painted. Check texture surfaces from different angles for a complete, uniform coverage.

Electrical

The following is a list of things to look for when installing or inspecting a contractor's electrical job.

○ Before the drywall is installed, make sure that outlet and switch boxes are positioned so the front edge of the box will be flush with the drywall. Look for overall neatness and a slight slack in all the wires–they should not be taunt.

○ Make sure all room outlet and lighting circuits provide at least 15 amp service. Outlets in the kitchen, home office, laundry room and workshop should be 20 amp service.

○ Electric outlets must at least be to code, but ideally they should be about 8 feet apart so that no lamp or appliance needs an extension cord. Make sure all outlets are properly grounded. Every room should have a light switch that operates either a permanent fixture or half of one outlet.

○ After any remodeling, make sure that the home's ground has not been interrupted by plumbing or other changes. Near any location that can become wet, such as bathroom, kitchen or laundry room, make sure ground fault circuit interrupters (GFCIs) are installed for all outlets to protect against shocks.

○ Hot tubs and whirlpools should also have a ground fault circuit interrupter specially made for high-amperage whirlpools. No switches or other electrical devices should be in reach of anyone in the whirlpool.

○ Electrical wiring that runs across an unfinished concrete wall in a garage, basement or any other location should be enclosed in metal conduit.

○ All bathrooms, new and remodeled, should have a ventilator fan.

○ There should be at least one smoke detector on every level of a home. Ideally, there should be one outside every bedroom, near the kitchen, near the laundry room, near the utility room, in the shop and at the top of all stairways.

○ Using a reliable circuit tester, check for proper voltage and grounding at all outlets. Use a voltmeter to check the lighting circuits. Test all ground fault circuit interrupters by pressing the test button. If the test button doesn't instantly stop the flow of electricity, it is faulty.

○ Make sure all lighting fixtures and ceiling fans are installed properly and securely. Make sure the bulb in each fixture doesn't exceed manufacturer's recommendations. Pay particular attention to recessed light fixtures. Heat can build up in recessed fixtures if the bulb is of too high a wattage.

○ Make sure all outlet and switch covers are in place. Test all regular and dimmer switches. Make sure all 3-way and 4-way switches work from every location and with every possible combination of switch settings.

○ Call for a final inspection. An experienced inspector may be able to spot troubles before they become dangerous.

Painting

The following is a list of things to look for when installing or inspecting a contractor's painting job.

○ Make sure all nicks, scratches, nail holes and other blemishes are spackled.

○ All new drywall must be primed with a heavy-body latex primer. In previously painted rooms, new spackling should be primed.

Choose the right finish coat for the room. Painted trim should be in gloss latex paint. The kitchen and bathroom should be in semi-gloss, which resists stains better than flat paint. Hallways and children's rooms can be painted in a new paint luster, sometimes called low-luster or eggshell or silk luster. This is less shiny than semi-gloss, yet more resistant to fingerprints than flat paint. Paint living rooms and bedrooms with flat paint. Although most paint companies sell a ceiling paint, use regular good-quality wall paint in a ceiling white color for any ceilings.

○ Paint should go on evenly and completely, yet without runs. If, after one coat, you can see places where the previous color comes through paint the entire room with a second coat. Applying a second coat to just some areas will show almost as much as the places you missed with the first coat. During or after painting, inspect all painted surfaces for drips, lap marks, roller ridges and brush marks. There shouldn't be any. Make sure that the borders with ceiling are neat and straight. Paint closets and the inside of cupboards.

○ Slip the foot from a pair of pantyhose over your hand and slide it along trim work. There should be no snags. Nail holes should be puttied. Trim should receive at least two coats of paint or varnish. Make sure closet shelves, cupboards and the inside of cabinets are finished.

○ Check trim, paneling, cabinetry, ceramic tile, hardware and countertops for paint runs, splatters or drips. Remove any.

○ If possible, return any unused gallons for a refund. Retain opened cans for touch ups.

○ If the color doesn't seem to match what you wanted on the color sample, wait at least two days before deciding to repaint. This isn't a technical aspect. Another coat can go on relatively soon. But paint colors change while they dry and they change with different light. Make sure the paint that doesn't look right to you initially really is wrong before changing it.

○ Write the date and the name of the room on an adhesive label and put it on the top of the paint can. Write the brand of paint, the type of luster and the name or number of the paint on an adhesive label and put in on the back side of the main light switch to the room. This way you'll know what paints go with what rooms and you can get replacement paint easily, if you need it.

Plumbing

The following is a list of things to look for when installing or inspecting a contractor's plumbing job.

○ Make sure the main water supply shut-off valve is easily accessible and works to shut off the water completely.

○ If extra roof vents were installed for drain vents, check the roof for proper vent flashing.

○ Before attaching a fiberglass bath tub into place, stand in the tub in stocking feet in the spot where it will be installed. Make sure it doesn't rock. Check to see if the bottom flexes when you get in and out. If it does, it will probably make a noise. This is an indication that the tub will, over time, crack from the flexing and leak. Better tubs shouldn't flex. The best way to install any fiberglass tub or shower stall is to fill the area below the base with sand mix concrete. The concrete will strengthen the base of the tub.

○ Check the tub, shower stall, toilet, sink and ceramic tile for any chipping, flaws or damage to the finish.

○ Make sure the water heater is set securely and doesn't rock. If it's a gas water heater, make sure the exhaust vent is complete and rises from the top of the water heater.

○ For all showers and tubs use only scald-proof single-handle faucets. These faucets prevent anyone from accidentally turning on only hot water and scalding skin. Make sure that when you turn on the scald-proof faucets, it is cold water that comes out first and gradually moves to hotter water, not the other way around.

○ Make sure the hot water is on the left and the cold water is on the right on all faucets.

○ Check all faucets to make sure the flow of water is ample and unrestricted. Check water pressure and volume by turning on all faucets and flushing the toilet. Any drop in pressure should be minimal and temporary.

○ Turn all faucets on and off quickly and listen for noisy vibrations in the pipe, commonly called "water hammers." Pipes that vibrate can be better secured, or an air damper can be installed to reduce this noise.

○ Check all drains for water flow with the faucets for the shower, tub and sinks wide open. None of them should fill up. Run water down each drain separately and listen carefully for bubbling or gurgling. This is indication of insufficient venting on these lines.

○ Call for a final inspection. An experienced inspector may be able to spot troubles before they cause expensive problems.

Trim

The following is a list of things to look for when installing or inspecting a contractor's job of installing trim.

○ Inspect all wood before installation and make sure it is trim grade and is free from blemishes or defects. Reject any piece that would make the project look sub-standard. Make sure it is of all the same wood. Even if stained, pine, oak and lauan (commonly called mahogany) will take stains differently and they have different grain patterns. If you can't tell the difference among these three woods readily, get someone who can.

○ Make sure all the pieces of the moldings are installed in the correct place, including base, base shoe, stops, chair rails and crown moldings. It is not unusual for professionals and do-it-yourselfers to forget a piece.

○ On hardwood or vinyl floors, install a quarter-round base shoe after the base-board molding has been stained and varnished. Nail it into the floor, not the baseboard, half way between floor joists. That way, if the floor sags slightly over time, there will not be a noticeable gap.

○ Make sure all joints are clean-cut and tight-fitting. Pay special attention to miter joints on the outside (convex) corners. Make sure all paneling is plumb so the grooves go straight up and down. Make sure shelves are secure and level. Make sure the fireplace mantel is level and secure.

○ All nails should be set below the trim surface and the divot should be puttied over with a quality putty that matches the surface. The trim surface should be free of hammer dents.

○ Make sure that all stair treads are solid and squeak-free. Hand rails and balusters should feel safe and secure when gripped. Remember, over time, these items will wear slightly on their fasteners. If they don't feel secure when new, they will be dangerous later on.

Doors

The following is a list of things to look for when installing or inspecting a contractor's job of installing doors.

○ Make sure all doors are the correct type and match the trim work and, if possible, match the cabinets and vanities.

○ Most doors should open into a smaller room, such as a bedroom or bathroom, from the larger room or hallway. (Except closets.) From inside the smaller room, check to see that the gap between the door and jamb is equal all the way around.

○ Door stops should be set so that the door closes snugly, but easily. The door should swing freely and quietly. The door should stay open at any angle without falling closed or open. The bottom of the door should be cut for a high enough clearance to pass easily over carpet or tile. To test this in a home without carpet, take a scrap of carpet and put in front of the door, then open it.

○ Door knobs, latches and hinges should work easily and look good. Latches should align with latch plates.

○ Door trim should be installed uniformly around the door jamb. Corner miters at the top corners should fit well. The nails should be countersunk and filled and there should be no hammer dents or splits.

○ On exterior doors, thresholds should be installed properly and adjusted so that they keep out wind and dust, but the doors open easily. All outside doors should be weather stripped. Before the inside molding is attached, the gaps between the exterior door jamb and the framing lumber should be filled or caulked. The joint of brick molding on the outside of the door where it meets the siding should be caulked.

○ All exterior doors should lock and almost all of them should be keyed. (Sliding glass doors are the exception because the auxiliary locks prevent many of them from opening with a key anyway.) All exterior doors should have deadbolt locks besides door knob locks for security. Each lock should be keyed alike so one key fits all.

Safety Procedures

Safety should always be the first consideration when working in the workshop. Woodworking involves techniques and equipment that, if improperly used, can lead to accidents. Fortunately, you can create a safe workshop environment and a method of working that permits both creative and safe work.

Before using tools and equipment, read the owner's manuals provided by the manufacturer and familiarize yourself with all safety features, procedures and warnings. Also, recognize and understand all parts and components of each tool in the workshop.

The size of a workshop and the type of woodworking performed directly affect workshop safety. Obviously, using a fretsaw to make marquetry is safer than using a table saw and sharper in a cabinet shop. However, there still are fundamental safety rules that should be followed. The following is a list of some general precautions and safety considerations for working in the workshop.

Safety Tips

1. Don't work on a project if you're tired. The U.S. military has found that fatigue is a key factor in most of its fatal accidents.

2. Never attempt a project if you are drinking alcohol or taking medications that can cause drowsiness or lack of concentration.

3. Don't wear loose fitting clothing. Baggy sleeves, neckties, scarves and open shirts and sweaters can get caught in tools and machinery.

4. Remove all jewelry, including rings and watches, and tie up long hair.

5. Don't work alone if you cannot readily summon help if there is an accident.

6. Electric tools should be unplugged when making adjustments or attaching accessories.

7. Do not work in a shop with a cluttered floor. It's too easy to trip or slip.

8. For best results–and safer fingers and hands–install proper lighting.

9. Never disregard hazard warnings or eliminate or override a tool's safety features.

10. Always read the labels before using cleaning solvents, finishing products and other chemicals.

11. Check to make sure the electrical service to the workshop is sufficient to operate all tools and machinery safely.

12. Never use a tool for a purpose other than what it is intended.

13. Be sure any modification to a tool is within the design limits of that tool.

14. Don't add an accessory to a tool if it is not acceptable or safe. Particularly, don't add home-made cutting heads to tools that spin.

15. Check with your homeowner's insurance agent regarding coverage for accidents in the workshop.

16. Keep emergency numbers near a workshop phone. If possible, program your telephone to call police, fire or 911 emergency numbers.

17. Finally, be informed, alert and conscious of safety at all times.

An accident can shorten a life or end a rewarding hobby. Remember, power tools can cut, twist and crush human body parts just as they do wood, steel and plastic. They require knowledge to operate. Don't be afraid or too proud to increase your knowledge. Read manuals, woodworking magazines and newspaper articles and watch home-repair TV shows and videos. Use safety guards, wear protective eyewear, never work when you're fatigued and keep up-to-date on safety procedures and hazardous materials.

Electrical Box Sizes

Two crucial pieces of electrical safety information is the maximum number of wires an electrical box will legally accommodate and the proper size of wire to be used.

The electrical box limit is based on the volume in cubic inches of the box. There must be adequate free space for all the conductors that will be enclosed.

Various Box Sizes and the Number of Wires They Will Hold

Type of box	Box size in inches		Maximum number of wires			
			#14	#12	#10	#8
Outlet box	4 x 1¼	Round	6	5	5	4
	4 x 1½	or	7	6	6	5
	4 x 2⅛	Octagonal	10	9	8	7
	4 x 1¼	Square	9	8	7	6
	4 x 1½	Square	10	9	8	7
	4 x 2⅛	Square	15	13	12	10
	4¹¹⁄₁₆ x 1¼	Square	12	11	10	8
	4¹¹⁄₁₆ x 1½	Square	14	13	11	9
	4¹¹⁄₁₆ x 2⅛	Square	21	18	16	14
Switch box	3 x 2 x 1		3	3	3	2
	3 x 2 x 2½		5	4	4	2
	3 x 2 x 2¼		5	4	4	3
	3 x 2 x 2½		6	5	5	4
	3 x 2 x 2¾		7	6	5	4
	3 x 2 x 3½		9	8	7	6
Handy box	4 x 2⅛ x 1½		5	4	4	3
	4 x 2⅛ x 1⅞		6	5	5	4
	4 x 2⅛ x 2⅛		7	6	5	4

Electrical boxes are available in varying depths. It costs very little to use a deeper box and the extra space makes it easier to fold the wires in place when installing switches, receptacles and light fixtures.

Ideally receptacles should be mounted 16 inches from the surface of the floor. Most codes require receptacles be spaced close enough together so that no distance along a wall is greater than 6 feet from an outlet.

128

Wire Sizes & Ratings

The size of an electrical cable is determined by its capacity to carry a maximum amount of current. American Wire Gauge (AWG) wire sizes are numbered–the smaller the number, the larger the wire. For instance, a regular light switch might be wired with #12 wire. An oven would require #8 or even #6.

Although cheaper, working with aluminum wire for regular household wiring may have some potential problems with certain switches and receptacles. If you aren't familiar with those potential problems, use copper wire.

The following chart is for the two most common types of wire used for electrical wiring in homes and commercial offices today. Type THHN wire, or equivalent, is for dry locations. Type XHHW wire, or equivalent, is for wet locations. The letters in the types of wire are not acronyms, but refer to properties of the insulation. THHN insulation is made from a fire-resistant, high-temperature thermoplastic. XHHW insulation is made from a fire-resistant, cross-linked synthetic polymer.

Most wires in a home will be in conduit or a cable jacket, which means in most cases you should use the lower amperage rating. All amperages are based on a maximum ambient temperature of 194° F (90° C). The amperage capacity is reduced by increased temperature or moisture.

Ampacity of copper and aluminum wire

AWG	Copper In cable, conduit or buried in earth	In free air	Aluminum In cable, conduit or buried in earth	In free air
16	18	24		
14	25 *	35 *		
12	30	40 *	25 *	35 *
10	40	55 *	35 *	40 *
8	55	80	45	60
6	75	105	60	80
4	95	140	75	110
3	110	165	85	130
2	130	190	100	150
1	150	220	115	170
1/0	170	260	135	205
2/0	195	300	150	235
3/0	225	350	175	275
4/0	260	405	205	315

* Higher amperage ratings are given in some code books, but these wire sizes should be used for protection against current overload.

Measurements & Conversions

Lumber

Widths: Individual metric cross-sections are considered equal to the nearest imperial size.

Lengths: Metric lengths are based on a 300 millimeter standard which is slightly shorter in length than a foot. It is important, therefore, to check your requirements accurately. Consult the nearest inch on the table below to locate the metric length required.

* A standard metric area is a square meter. Use the conversions shown below when converting from imperial measurements.

Metric Sizes Shown Beside Nearest Imperial Equivalent

mm	Inches	mm	Inches	mm	Inches	mm	Inches
16 x 75	⅝ x 3	44 x 150	1¾ x 6	25 x 300	1 x 12	63 x 225	2½ x 9
16 x 100	⅝ x 4	44 x 175	1¾ x 7	32 x 75	1¼ x 3	75 x 100	3 x 4
16 x 125	⅝ x 5	44 x 200	1¾ x 8	32 x 100	1¼ x 4	75 x 125	3 x 5
16 x 150	⅝ x 6	44 x 225	1¾ x 9	32 x 125	1¼ x 5	75 x 150	3 x 6
19 x 75	¾ x 3	44 x 250	1¾ x 10	32 x 150	1¼ x 6	75 x 175	3 x 7
19 x 100	¾ x 4	44 x 300	1¾ x 12	32 x 175	1¼ x 7	75 x 200	3 x 8
19 x 125	¾ x 5	50 x 75	2 x 3	32 x 200	1¼ x 8	75 x 225	3 x 9
19 x 150	¾ x 6	50 x 100	2 x 4	32 x 225	1¼ x 9	75 x 250	3 x10
22 x 75	⅞ x 3	50 x 125	2 x 5	32 x 250	1¼ x 10	75 x 300	3 x12
22 x 100	⅞ x 4	50 x 150	2 x 6	32 x 300	1¼ x 12	100 x 100	4 x 4
22 x 125	⅞ x 5	50 x 175	2 x 7	38 x 75	1½ x 3	100 x 150	4 x 6
22 x 150	⅞ x 6	50 x 200	2 x 8	38 x 100	1½ x 4	100 x 200	4 x 8
25 x 75	1 x 3	50 x 225	2 x 9	38 x 125	1½ x 5	100 x 250	4 x 10
25 x 100	1 x 4	50 x 250	2 x 10	38 x 150	1½ x 6	100 x 300	4 x 12
25 x 125	1 x 5	50 x 300	2 x 12	38 x 175	1½ x 7	150 x 150	6 x 6
25 x 150	1 x 6	63 x 100	2½ x 4	38 x 200	1½ x 8	150 x 200	6 x 8
25 x 175	1 x 7	63 x 125	2½ x 5	38 x 225	1½ x 9	150 x 300	6 x 12
25 x 200	1 x 7	63 x 150	2½ x 6	44 x 75	1¾ x 3	200 x 200	8 x 8
25 x 225	1 x 7	63 x 175	2½ x 7	44 x 100	1¾ x 4	250 x 250	10 x 10
25 x 250	1 x 7	63 x 200	2½ x 8	44 x 125	1¾ x 5	300 x 300	12 x 12

Converting English to Metric

Inches x 25.4 = millimeters

Feet x .3048 = meters

Miles x 1.6093 = kilometers

Square inches x 6.4515 = square centimeters

Square feet x .09290 = square meters

Cubic inches x 16.3872 = cubic centimeters

Cubic feet x .02832 = cubic meters

Cubic yards x .76452 = cubic meters

Ounces x 28.35 = grams

Pounds x .4536 = kilograms

Tons (2,000 lbs.) x .9072 = metric tons

Horsepower x.746 = kilowatts

Converting Metric to English

Millimeters x .03937 = inches

Meters x 3.2809 = feet

Kilometers x.62138 = miles

Square centimeters x .155 = square inches

Square meters x 10.7641 = square feet

Cubic centimeters x .06103 = cubic inches

Cubic meters x 35.314 = cubic feet

Cubic meters x 1.308 = cubic yards

Grams x .03527 = ounces

Kilograms x 2.2046 = pounds

Metric tons x 1.1023 = tons (2,000 pounds)

Kilowatts x 1.3405 = horsepower

Metric Lengths

Metric lengths are based on a 300 millimeter standard which is slightly shorter in length than a foot. It is important, therefore, to check your requirements accurately. Consult the nearest inch on the table below to locate the metric length required.

Length Meters	Equivalent Ft. & Inches
1.8m	5' 10⅞"
2.1m	6'10⅝"
2.4m	7' 10½"
2.7m	8' 10¼"
3.0m	9' 10⅛"
3.3m	10' 9⅞"
3.6m	11' 9¾"
3.9m	12' 9½"
4.2m	13' 9⅜"
4.5m	14' 9⅓"
4.8m	15' 9"
5.1m	16' 8¾"
5.4m	17' 8⅝"
5.7m	18' 8⅜"
6.0m	19' 8¼"
6.3m	20' 8"
6.6m	21' 7⅞"
6.9m	22' 7⅝"
7.2m	23' 7½"
7.5m	24'7¼"
7.8m	25' 7⅛"

All the dimensions are based on 1 inch = 25 mm.

131

Nail Sizes

Nails – Number Per Pound

Size	Weight Unit	Common	Casing	Box	Finishing
2d	Pound	876	1010	1010	1351
3d	Pound	586	635	635	807
4d	Pound	316	473	473	548
5d	Pound	271	406	406	500
6d	Pound	181	236	236	309
7d	Pound	161	210	210	238
8d	Pound	106	145	145	189
9d	Pound	96	132	132	172
10d	Pound	69	94	94	121
12d	Pound	64	88	88	113
16d	Pound	49	71	71	90
20d	Pound	31	52	52	62

Actual Size

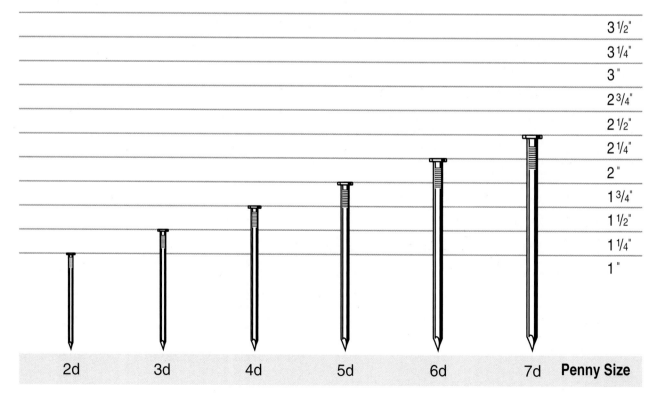

Nails – Length and Diameter in Inches and Centimeters

| | Length | | Diameter | |
Size	Inches	Centimeters	Inches	Centimeters
2d	1	2.5	.068	.17
3d	1¼	3.2	.102	.26
4d	1½	3.8	.102	.26
5d	1¾	4.4	.102	.26
6d	2	5.1	.115	.29
7d	2¼	5.7	.115	.29
8d	2½	6.4	.131	.33
9d	2¾	7.0	.131	.33
10d	3	7.6	.148	.38
12d	3¼	8.3	.148	.38
16d	3½	8.9	.148	.38
20d	4	10.2	.203	.51

Actual Size

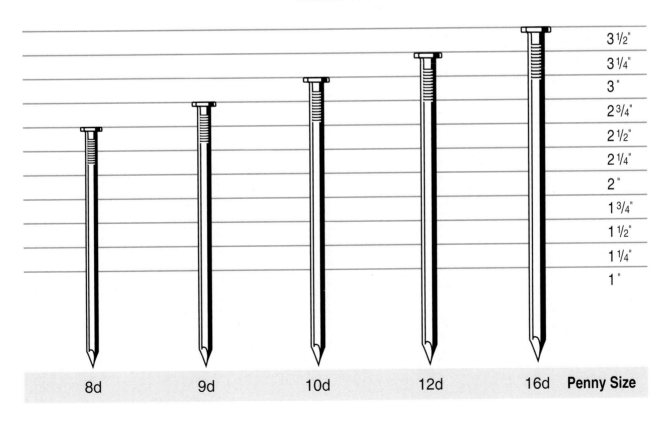

3½"
3¼"
3"
2¾"
2½"
2¼"
2"
1¾"
1½"
1¼"
1"

8d   9d   10d   12d   16d   **Penny Size**

133

Wood Screws

	Wood Screws				
Screws Gauge No.	Nominal Diameter		Length		
	Inches	mm	Inches	mm	
0	0.060	1.52	³⁄₁₆	4.8	
1	0.070	1.78	¼	6.4	
2	0.082	2.08	⁵⁄₁₆	7.9	
3	0.094	2.39	³⁄₈	9.5	
4	0.0108	2.74	⁷⁄₁₆	11.1	
5	0.122	3.10	½	12.7	
6	0.136	3.45	⁵⁄₈	15.9	
7	0.150	3.81	¾	19.1	
8	0.164	4.17	⁷⁄₈	22.2	
9	0.178	4.52	1	25.4	
10	0.192	4.88	¹⁄₁₄	31.8	
12	0.220	5.59	¹⁄₁₂	38.1	
14	0.248	6.30	1¾	44.5	
16	0.276	7.01	2	50.8	
18	0.304	7.72	2¼	57.2	
20	0.332	8.43	2½	63.5	
24	0.388	9.86	2¾	69.9	
28	0.444	11.28	3	76.2	
32	0.5	12.7	3¼	82.6	

Actual Size

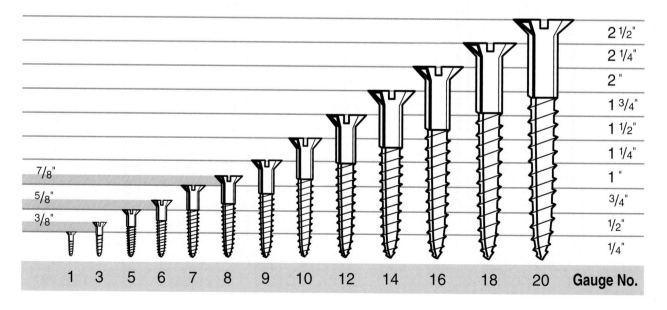

Types of Screws and Bolts

Screws

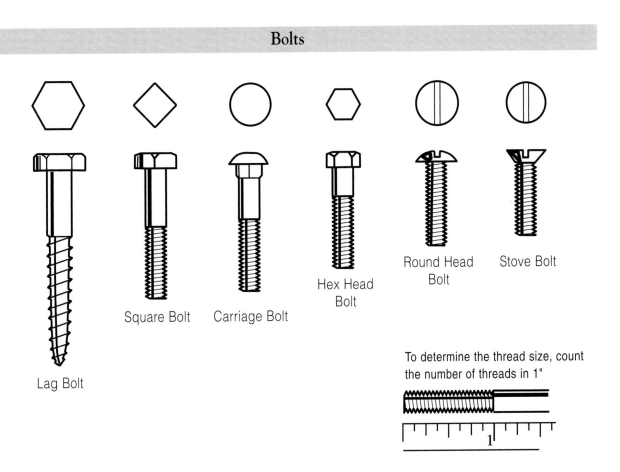

Flat Head
Wood Screw

Round Head
Wood Screw

Oval Head
Wood Screw

Oven Head
Machine Screw

Oval Head
Machine Screw

Sheet Metal
Screw

Bolts

Lag Bolt

Square Bolt

Carriage Bolt

Hex Head
Bolt

Round Head
Bolt

Stove Bolt

To determine the thread size, count
the number of threads in 1"

1

135

Common Woods

Name of Wood	Hardness	Strength	Stability	Weight	Rot	Split	Work Quality for hand	Shaping	Turning	Mortising	Planing and Joining	Nailing	Gluing	Sanding	Cost
Alder	medium	weak	G	light	F	F	G	F	F	F	G	G	G	F	medium
Ash, white	medium	medium	E	medium heavy	F	G	P	E	F	F	G	G	F	E	medium
Balsa	soft	weak	G	light	P	E	E	P	P	P	G	E	E	P	low
Basswood	soft	weak	G	light	P	E	E	P	P	F	G	E	E	P	medium
Beech	hard	medium	P	heavy	P	G	F	F	F	G	F	P	G	G	medium
Birch	hard	strong	G	heavy	P	G	P	E	G	E	G	P	F	F	high
Butternut	soft	weak	E	light	F	F	G	F	G	F	G	F	G	F	medium
Cedar, red	soft	weak	G	medium	E	P	G	P	P	F	F	P	G	P	medium
Cherry	medium	medium	G	heavy	F	P	G	E	E	E	E	F	E	E	high
Chestnut	soft	weak	E	light	E	P	G	G	E	G	G	G	E	E	high
Cottonwood	soft	weak	G	light	P	E	E	P	P	P	G	E	E	P	low
Cypress	soft	medium	G	light	E	F	F	P	P	P	G	F	F	F	medium
Elm	medium	medium	P	medium heavy	F	G	F	P	P	G	P	E	F	G	medium
Fir, Douglas	medium	medium strong	F	medium heavy	G	F	F	P	P	G	G	G	G	F	medium
Fir, white		low		light	G	G	G	P	P	G	G	G	G	G	low
Gum, red	medium	medium	P	medium	F	G	G	F	E	F	F	G	E	F	medium
Hickory	hard	strong	G	heavy	P	F	P	F	G	E	G	P	G	E	medium
Lauan	medium	medium	E	medium	G	P	G	F	G	F	G	G	E	P	medium
Magnolia	soft	weak	F	medium	F	G	G	G	F	P	G	E	E	G	medium
Mahogany	medium	medium	E	medium heavy	F	P	G	E	E	E	G	G	E	G	high
Maple, hard	hard	strong	G	heavy	P	P	P	E	E	E	F	P	F	G	high
Maple, soft	medium	medium	F	medium	F	G	G	F	F	P	P	F	G	G	medium
Oak, red	hard	strong	E	heavy	P	F	P	F	G	E	E	G	G	E	medium
Oak, white	hard	strong	E	heavy	F	F	P	G	G	E	E	G	G	E	high
Pine, ponderosa	soft	weak	G	light	F	P	E	G	G	F	G	E	E	F	low
Pine, sugar	soft	weak	G	light	F	P	E	G	G	F	G	E	E	P	low
Pine, white	soft	weak	G	light	F	P	E	G	G	F	G	E	E	G	low
Pine, yellow	hard	strong	F	heavy	G	P	F	G	P	G	G	F	F	F	medium
Poplar	soft	weak	G	medium	P	G	E	P	G	F	G	E	E	P	medium
Redwood	soft	medium	E	medium	E	G	G	G	F	P	G	G	E	P	medium
Spruce	soft	weak	G	light	F	F	G	G	G	F	G	G	G	G	medium
Sycamore	medium	medium	P	heavy	F	G	G	P	G	E	P	E	G	P	medium
Walnut	medium	strong	E	heavy	G	F	G	E	G	E	E	G	F	E	high
Willow	soft	weak	G	light	G	G	G	F	F	F	F	G	G	G	low

(E=Excellent, G=Good, F=Fair, P=Poor)

136

Sizing and Squaring

Board Sizes

Nominal Size (This is what you order.) Inches	Actual Size (This is what you get.) Inches
1 x 1"	¾ x ¾"
1 x 2"	¾ x 1½"
1 x 3"	¾ x 2½"
1 x 4"	¾ x 3½"
1 x 6"	¾ x 5½"
1 x 8"	¾ x 7¼"
1 x 10"	¾ x 9¼"
1 x 12"	¾ x 11¼"
2 x 2"	1¾ x 1¾"
2 x 3"	1½ x 2½"
2 x 4"	1½ x 3½"
2 x 6"	1½ x 5½"
2 x 8"	1½ x 7¼"
2 x 10"	1½ x 9¼"
2 x 12"	1½ x 11¼"
3 x 4"	2½ x 11¼"
4 x 4"	3½ x 3½"
4 x 6"	3½ x 5½"
6 x 6"	5½ x 5½"
8 x 8"	7¼ x 7¼"

Keep Large Projects Square with Pythagorean

When building a deck or any large rectangular structure, you can make sure the corners are square by using the carpenters' 3-4-5 method, otherwise known as the Pythagorean Theorem. Start by driving a corner stake. Then tie two pieces of string to the stake. Measure out on either string a distance of 3' and mark the string at that point. Then measure out 4' on the other string, and mark the string at that point. Move the two strings apart until the distance between the marks on the two strings is 5' Drive stakes to hold the two lines in this position. This corner is now square. The Pythagorean Theorem states that in order for an angle to be 90 degrees, a triangular line opposite that angle, or the hypotenuse, is equal to the sum of the squares of the other two sides. Or, 3 x 3 + 4 x 4 = 5 x 5, or 9 + 16 = 25. For even larger projects, you can double this formula. Or, 6 x 6 + 8 x 8 = 10 x 10, or 36 + 64 = 100. When laying out a deck from a home, start at one deck corner next to the house to create a line that is 90 degrees to the house and then figure the other line from this existing one.

Formula: $a^2 + b^2 = c^2$

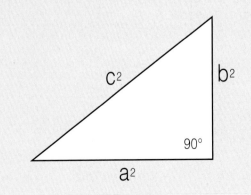

Compound Cuts

Cutting Compound Angles with Power Tools

Compound cuts on a table saw are done by establishing both a miter gauge setting and a blade tilt. (See Figure.) It's critical that settings for both of these angles be accurate. A slight error is multiplied by the number of sides or joints. Two degrees of error per cut compounds to a total of 16 degrees with just four sides. The accompanying chart tells what the blade tilt and miter gauge must be set at for most commonly used angles. Some of these settings are to a fraction of a degree and you won't find that kind of precision marked on most table saws. Test cuts and accurate angle gauge are in order before sawing good stock. When the work is too wide for crosscutting with a miter gauge, make the cuts with a taper jig. This accessory is available for most saws.

Work Slope Angle	4-Sided Figure		6-Sided Figure		8-Sided Figure	
	Blade	Miter Gauge	Blade	Miter Gauge	Blade	Miter Gauge
10 degrees	44¼	80¼	29½	84¼	22	86
20 degrees	41¾	71¼	28¼	79	21	82
30 degrees	37¾	63½	26	74	19½	78¼
40 degrees	32½	57¼	22¾	69¾	17	75
50 degrees	27	52½	19	66¼	14½	72½
60 degrees	21	49	14½	63½	11	70¼

Compound Cuts On a Radial Arm Saw

Radial arm saws are commonly thought of as cross-cut saws, but they are very versatile. Compound cuts on a radial arm saw require swinging the arm for the miter setting and tilting the blade for the bevel. Correct settings for most commonly used slopes are listed here. One easy way is to cut similar pieces consecutively from the same board. First make an end cut and then flip the board for additional cuts. A stop block on the fence can be used to control the length of these pieces.

Work Slope Angle	4-Sided Figure		6-Sided Figure		8-Sided Figure	
	Blade	Miter Gauge	Blade	Miter Gauge	Blade	Miter Gauge
10 degrees	44¼	9¼	29½	5½	22	4
20 degrees	41¾	18¼	28¼	11	21	8
30 degrees	37¾	26½	26	16	19½	11¾
40 degrees	32½	32¼	22¾	20¼	17	15
50 degrees	27	37½	19	23¾	14¼	17½
60 degrees	21	41	14½	26½	11	19¾

Common Grades of Plywood

Grade (exterior)	Face	Back	Inner plies	Uses
Exterior				
A-A	A	A	C	Outdoors, where durability and appearance of both surfaces are important.
A-B	A	B	C	Alternate for A-A, where appearance of one side is not important but the face surface is of finish grade.
A-C	A	C	C	Soffits, fences and base for coatings.
B-C	B	C	C	For utilitarian purposes such as farm buildings, some fences and base coatings.
303 Siding	C (or better)	C	C	Each panel has varying surface textures and grooving patterns. Good for siding, fences, paneling, screens, etc.
T1-11	C	C	C	A special plywood of 5/8 inch thick panels with deep parallel grooves. Available in textured, unsanded or Medium-Density-Overlay surfaces.
C-C (plugged)	C (plugged)	C	C	Use as base for tile and linoleum installation or backing for wall coverings.
C-C	C	C	C	Unsanded. Good for backing and rough construction if exposed to weather.
B-B Plyform	B	B	C	Use for concrete forms. It is possible to reuse panels until worn out.
MDO	B	B or C	C	Medium-Density-Overlay (MDO) is ideal base for paint, siding, built-ins and signs and displays.
HDO	A or B	A or B	C-plugged or C	High-Density-Overlay (HDO) is good for hard surfaces such as unpainted concrete forms, cabinets, counter tops and tanks.

				Interior
Grade (interior)	Face	Back	Inner plies	Uses
A-A	A	A	D	Good for cabinet doors, built-ins and furniture where both sides will show.
A-B	A	B	D	Good alternate for A-A if finish grade is needed for only one side yet a solid and relatively good side is needed for the other.
A-D	A	D	D	A good quality finish-grade for paneling and built-ins
B-D	B	D	D	Sheathing and structural uses and temporary purposes.
C-D	C	D	D	For use under tile and carpeting.
Underlayment	C-plugged	D	C^1 and D	Ideal for combinations of subfloor and underlayment, under tile and carpeting.
Sturd-1-Floor	C-plugged	D	C^1 and D	

How Bricks Are Sized

Most bricks aren't made to exacting specifications, so they're usually referred to by nominal dimensions instead of their actual size, just like lumber. Just as the standard 2"x4" is really 1½"x3 ½", bricks are also a bit smaller than their listed dimensions. But this nominal sizing is very convenient for figuring out how many bricks you'll need.

The nominal size of a brick is the actual size of the brick plus the width of the mortar joint. Bricks are installed using ⅜" or ½" mortar joints. Today, ½" joints are the most popular. When buying brick, specify the nominal size plus the mortar joint thickness you will be using. For instance, the nominal size of common brick is 2⅔"x4"x8". For ⅜" joints, brick makers make the actual size of common brick 2¼" x 3⅝" x 7⅝". For ½" joints,

brick makers make the actual size of common bricks 2¼" x 3½" x 7½". Note that the 2⅔" nominal height measurement is about halfway between the 2⅝" and 2¾" actual heights per course (layer) created with ⅜" and ½" mortar joints.

The first of the accompanying tables lists the nominal dimensions of popular brick types plus their actual dimensions for use with ⅜" and ½ " mortar joints. The other two tables list the wall heights created by courses using common brick and ½" and ⅜" mortar joints.

Commonly Used Brick

Brick Type	Nominal Dimensions HxWxL	Mortar Joint thickness	Actual Dimensions HxWxL
Common	2⅔ x 4 x 8	⅜	2¼ x 3⅝ x 7⅝
		½	2¼ x 3½ x 7½
Norman	2⅔ x 4 x 12	⅜	2¼ x 3⅝ x 11⅝
		½	2¼ x 3½ x 11½
Roman	2 x 4 x 12	⅜	1⅝ x 3⅝ x 11⅝
		½	1½ x 3½ x 11½
Baby Roman	2 x 4 x 8	⅜	1⅝ x 3⅝ x 7⅝
		½	1½ x 3½ x 7½
SCR	2⅔ x 6 x 12	⅜	2¼ x 5⅝ x 11⅝
		½	2¼ x 5½ x 11½
Economy	4 x 4 x 12	⅜	3⅝ x 3⅝ x 11⅝
		½	3½ x 3½ x 11½
Jumbo Six	4 x 6 x 12	⅜	3⅝ x 5⅝ x 11⅝
		½	3½ x 5½ x 11½
Jumbo Eight	4 x 8 x 12	⅜	3⅝ x 7⅝ x 11⅝
		½	3½ x 7½ x 11½

Nominal Heights of Common Brick Walls

Using ½" Mortar Joints				Using ⅜" Mortar Joints			
Courses	Height	Courses	Height	Courses	Height	Courses	Height
1	2¾"	26	5' - 11½"	1	2⅝"	26	5' - 8¼"
2	5½"	27	6' - 2¼"	2	5¼"	27	5' - 10⅞"
3	8¼"	28	6' - 5"	3	7⅞"	28	6' - 1½"
4	11"	29	6' - 7¾"	4	10½"	29	6' - 4¾"
5	1' - 1¾"	30	6' - 10½"	5	1' - 1⅛"	30	6' - 6¾"
6	1' - 4½"	31	7' - 1¼"	6	1' - 3¾"	31	6' - 9⅜"
7	1' - 7¼"	32	7' - 4"	7	1' - 6⅜"	32	7' - 0"
8	1' - 10"	33	7' - 6¾"	8	1' - 9"	33	7' - 2⅝"
9	2' - ¾"	34	7' - 9½"	9	1' - 11⅝"	34	7' - 5¼"
10	2' - 3½"	35	8' - ¼"	10	2' - 2¼"	35	7' - 7⅞"
11	2' - 6¼"	36	8' - 3"	11	2' - 4⅞"	36	7' - 10½"
12	2' - 9"	37	8' - 5¾"	12	2' - 7½"	37	8' - 1⅛"
13	2' - 11¾"	38	8' - 8½"	13	2' - 10⅛"	38	8' - 3¾"
14	3' - 2½"	39	8' - 11¼"	14	3' - ¾"	39	8' - 6⅜"
15	3' - 5¼"	40	9' - 2"	15	3' - 3⅜"	40	8' - 9"
16	3' - 8"	41	9' - 4¾"	16	3' - 6"	41	8' - 11⅝"
17	3' - 10¾"	42	9' - 7½"	17	3' - 8⅝"	42	9' - 2¼"
18	4' - 1½"	43	9' - 10¼"	18	3' - 11¼"	43	9' - 4⅞"
19	4' - 4¼"	44	10' - 1"	19	4' - 1⅞"	44	9' - 7½"
20	4' - 7"	45	10' - 3¾"	20	4' - 4½"	45	9' - 10⅛"
21	4' - 9¾"	46	10' - 6½"	21	4' - 7⅛"	46	10' - ¾"
22	5' - ½"	47	10' - 9¼"	22	4' - 9¾"	47	10' - 3⅜"
23	5' - 3¼"	48	11' - 0"	23	5' - ⅜"	48	10' - 6"
24	5' - 6"	49	11' - 2¾"	24	5' - 3"	49	10' - 8⅝"
25	5' - 8¾"	50	11' - 5½"	25	5' - 5⅝"	50	10' - 11¼"

Wood Stove & Fireplace Tips

Wood stoves add a functional improvement to most homes, in that you can heat with wood instead of electricity or natural gas, and they add a degree of charm no other furnace can match.

Tips on Using Your Wood Stove

Some wood stoves burn wood more efficiently than others. The workmanship and design of a stove are the most important features that affect efficiency. If possible, get a stove with a catalytic combustor. A catalytic combustor increases efficiency and reduces pollutants going up the chimney and into the air. If you plan to use an older stove, consider installing an after market catalytic combustor. Most new stoves are tested and rated for combustion efficiency. Compare the efficiencies of different stoves when purchasing this major appliance. Make sure your stove fits where you plan to put it. Many stoves look smaller in the dealer's showroom than they do in your home. Stack milk crates or boxes to simulate the size and try walking around the room. Consider buying a wood-burning cook stove. Some models are very attractive and have the advantage of saving on cooking fuel costs as well as providing room heat. Choose a wood stove with a flat top where a pan or old coffee pot of water can simmer during the day. It will add needed humidity to your room.

When starting a stove fire, use paper, slender sticks of kindling and one or two pieces of split wood. If the stove is smoking or downdrafting, add more paper. Paper burns quickly and creates the necessary heat to get a good updraft. Open all the flues and vents, get a good fire going and add more wood when your "starter set" has become a bed of coals. Then adjust the vents and flues. Add more wood when each fire is reduced to coals. Do not use lighter fluid, gasoline, or other flammables to start an indoor stove fire. Newspaper "logs" work well when used in combination with split firewood.

In a well-made, cast-iron wood stove, a single piece of wood smoldering on a bed of hot coals can still put out a lot of warmth. Coals will spring to a blaze even after several hours when you open the vents and add a little oxygen from the outside. Wood stoves heat a home best when they're near the center of the first floor, or in the basement or cellar.

HOW TO CHOOSE FIREWOODS

The Good Woods

BTUs per cord (in thousands)

Type of Tree

Type of Tree	BTUs	Type of Tree	BTUs
Shagbark Hickory	24,000	Beech	21,800
Black Locust	24,000	Yellow Birch	21,300
Ironwood (Hardback)	24,100	Sugar Maple	21,300
Apple	23,877	Red Oak	21,300
Rock Elm	23,488	White Ash	20,000
White Oak	22,700		

Second Choice Woods

BTUs per cord (in thousands)

Type of Tree

Black Walnut 19,500	Pitch Pine 17,970
White Birch 18,900	Sycamore 17,950
Black Cherry 18,770	Black Ash 17,300
Tamarack (Larch) 18,650	American Elm 17,200
Red Maple 18,600	Silver Maple 17,000
Green Ash 18,360	

Hardly Worthwhile Cutting

BTUs per cord (in thousands)

Type of Tree

Red Spruce 13,632	Aspen (Poplar) 2,500
Hemlock 13,500	White Pine 12,022
Black Willow 13,206	Basswood 11,700
Butternut 12,800	Balsam Fir 11,282
Red Pine 12,765	

The Best Way to Caulk

All exterior joints between siding and windows, doors, and masonry should be caulked with a good quality acrylic latex or silicone caulk. Acrylic latex is usually easier to use and can easily be painted. Silicone lasts longer. The price of the caulk usually reflects its life expectancy. More expensive caulks are usually rated for 25 to 50 years. You'll be re-painting before then and will have the opportunity to repair or recaulk at that point. With modern house paint lasting at least 10 years, if properly applied, don't get anything that can't last 1.5 times that long.

Caulk is sold in cartridges. It is applied with inexpensive metal caulk guns. Buy a gun with top and bottom supporting bars, rather than ones that are half rounds. These last longer and require less effort. One tube of caulk will fill about 25 feet of ¼" cracks or seal two small windows. If you have gaps larger than ¼", buy a foam backing cord to fill the gap. This may sound like an additional purchase, but it will save you the cost of filling large cracks with caulk, which is more expensive than the backer. If you buy caulk on sale, purchase more than you'll need. Unopened caulk has a long shelf life. Just like paint, sometimes caulk requires touch ups and this way you'll have tubes of matching caulk. Before you begin, check the label and buy the appropriate solvent needed for clean up. Many caulks clean up with soap and water. Paper towels are a necessity.

How to Make Beading Look Professional

Step 1: Pick a nice warm day. The ideal temperature for caulking is between 50° and 80° F. Wear grubby work clothes. Caulk doesn't come out of clothing well.

Step 2: Scrape out old caulk from the joint with a scraper. Brush dirt away with an old paint brush. Wipe the joint with a wet cloth and allow it to dry.

Step 3: Cut the tip of the nozzle to a 45-degree angle with a utility knife. The nozzles are marked with several lines showing different-size openings. The size of the opening dictates the size of the bead. Choose the smallest mark. It's always easier to go slow to fill a gap, rather than having caulk coming out all over everything. A wire coat hanger, cut with a pair of pliers, will go through the tip and break the seal at the end of the tube. Better caulk guns come with a seal piercer.

Step 4: Load the caulk gun by pulling the plunger rod, which is above the pistol grip, all the way back. Insert the cartridge into the gun so the cartridge nozzle faces out the front like the barrel of a gun. On one type of caulk gun, the plunger rod is engaged by turning it until the notched side faces down. The better caulk guns don't need to have the rods turned. Gently pull the trigger until you feel resistance.

Step 5: Place the caulk tube nozzle in the joint, and gently squeeze the trigger while pushing the tube away from you to fill the gap. Squeezing the trigger gently allows you to work at your own pace. If a gap appears in the bead of caulk, simply go back to where the gap began and continue. When you reach the end of the crack or joint, release pressure on the tube by releasing the plunger rod to stop the caulk from coming out.

Step 6: After creating a bead of caulk, complete the joint by smoothing it with your index finger. Wet your finger with water and run your wet finger over the joint. This should neaten the caulk line and gently push the caulk further into the gap.

Step 7: From more than a few feet away, no one will notice even a poor caulk bead. But near the front door, garage door and other very noticeable places, it's best to use masking tape to determine the edges of the caulk bead. Put pieces of mask-ing tape on each side. Apply the bead of caulk and smooth as before. Some will go on to the masking tape. Then, right away, remove the masking tape and using a clean wet finger, smooth the bead one last time.

Step 8: Clean up any excess caulk.

Choosing a Caulk

Type	Cost	Ease of Application	Durability	Paint Holding Ability
Acrylic latex	Medium	Easy	Very good	Good
Butyl	Medium	Hard	Good	Good
Foam-in-place	Low	Hard	Good*	Good
Latex	Low	Easy	Poor	Good
Oil	Low	Easy	Poor	Good/prime
Paintable silicone	High	Moderate	Very good	Good/prime
Polyurethane	Medium	Moderate	Excellent	Good
Silicone	High	Moderate	Excellent	Poor
Synthetic rubber	Medium	Hard	Good	Good/prime

*Use to fill large gaps and wall cavities; don't use outside without painting.

How Much Paint Do I Need?

A gallon of good-quality paint will cover 300 sq. ft. If you're covering dark surfaces with a light color or trying to hide any bright color, two coats will probably be needed. If that's the case, it's usually cheaper and better to paint first with a tinted latex primer and then follow with a finish coat.

Estimating the amount of paint you need isn't difficult. Try to err on the high side. It's better to have an extra gallon for touch ups rather than using every last drop. If you're tinting the final coat, buy it all together. Although most modern tinting methods are accurate, different people doing the tinting can make minor variations in the color. If there is any question, buy a resealable five gallon white bucket and mix all the paint together in it.

To figure the amount of paint needed, calculate the area of the walls and subtract the area of the doors and windows. To find the wall area, add the lengths of the walls to figure the perimeter. Then multiply this figure by the ceiling height. From this total area subtract about 20 sq. ft. for each door and 15 sq. ft. for each average window. The result will be the actual area you have to paint. Divide this total by 300 to find the number of gallons you need. Invariably, this number will end in a fraction. Remember paint comes only in quarts and gallons, so round up to nearest quart, remembering that a quart usually costs about as much as half a gallon. Always leave some extra for touch-ups.

To use the charts, find the width of your room along the left side of the table (vertical column). Then find the length of your room along the bottom (horizontal row). Read the number of gallons from the table where the row and column intersect. Round up to gallons and quarts as we explained.

Paint Allowance for Walls

	8	9	10	11	12	13	14	15	16	17	18	19	20	21	22	23	24
20	1.5	1.6	1.7	1.7	1.8	1.8	1.9	2.0	2.0	2.1	2.1	2.2	2.3	2.3	2.4	2.4	2.5
19	1.5	1.5	1.6	1.7	1.7	1.8	1.8	1.9	2.0	2.0	2.1	2.1	2.2	2.3	2.3	2.4	2.4
18	1.4	1.5	1.5	1.6	1.7	1.7	1.8	1.8	1.9	2.0	2.0	2.1	2.1	2.2	1.3	2.3	2.4
17	1.4	1.4	1.5	1.5	1.6	1.7	1.7	1.8	1.8	1.8	2.0	2.0	2.1	2.1	2.2	2.3	2.3
16	1.3	1.4	1.4	1.5	1.5	1.6	1.7	1.7	1.8	1.8	1.9	2.0	2.0	2.1	2.1	2.2	2.3
15	1.2	1.3	1.4	1.4	1.5	1.5	1.6	1.7	1.7	1.8	1.8	1.9	2.0	2.0	2.1	2.1	2.2
14	1.2	1.2	1.3	1.4	1.4	1.5	1.5	1.6	1.7	1.7	1.8	1.8	1.9	2.0	2.0	2.1	2.1
13	1.1	1.2	1.2	1.3	1.4	1.4	1.5	1.5	1.6	1.7	1.7	1.8	1.8	1.9	2.0	2.0	2.1
12	1.1	1.1	1.2	1.2	1.3	1.4	1.4	1.5	1.5	1.6	1.7	1.7	1.8	1.8	1.9	2.0	2.0
11	1.0	1.1	1.1	1.2	1.2	1.3	1.4	1.4	1.5	1.5	1.6	1.7	1.7	1.8	1.8	1.9	2.0
10	0.9	1.0	1.1	1.1	1.2	1.2	1.3	1.4	1.4	1.5	1.5	1.6	1.7	1.7	1.8	1.8	1.9
9	0.9	0.9	1.0	1.1	1.1	1.2	1.2	1.3	1.4	1.4	1.5	1.5	1.6	1.7	1.7	1.8	1.8
8	0.8	0.9	0.9	1.0	1.1	1.1	1.2	1.2	1.3	1.4	1.4	1.5	1.5	1.6	1.7	1.7	1.8
7	0.8	0.8	0.9	0.9	1.0	1.1	1.1	1.2	1.2	1.3	1.4	1.4	1.5	1.5	1.6	1.7	1.7
6	0.7	0.8	0.8	0.9	0.9	1.0	1.1	1.1	1.2	1.2	1.3	1.4	1.4	1.5	1.5	1.6	1.7

Paint Allowance for Ceilings

WIDTH \ LENGTH	8	9	10	11	12	13	14	15	16	17	18	19	20	21	22	23	24
20	0.5	0.6	0.7	0.7	0.8	0.9	0.9	1.0	1.1	1.1	1.2	1.3	1.3	1.4	1.5	1.5	1.6
19	0.5	0.6	0.6	0.7	0.8	0.8	0.9	1.0	1.0	1.1	1.1	1.2	1.3	1.3	1.4	1.5	1.5
18	0.5	0.5	0.6	0.7	0.7	0.8	0.8	0.9	1.0	1.0	1.1	1.1	1.2	1.3	1.3	1.4	1.4
17	0.5	0.5	0.6	0.6	0.7	0.7	0.8	0.9	0.9	1.0	1.0	1.1	1.1	1.2	1.2	1.3	1.4
16	0.4	0.5	0.5	0.6	0.6	0.7	0.7	0.8	0.9	0.9	1.0	1.0	1.1	1.1	1.2	1.2	1.3
15	0.4	0.5	0.5	0.6	0.6	0.7	0.7	0.8	0.8	0.9	0.9	1.0	1.0	1.1	1.1	1.2	1.2
14	0.4	0.4	0.5	0.5	0.6	0.6	0.7	0.7	0.7	0.8	0.8	0.9	0.9	1.0	1.0	1.1	1.1
13	0.3	0.4	0.4	0.5	0.5	0.6	0.6	0.7	0.7	0.7	0.8	0.8	0.9	0.9	1.0	1.0	1.0
12	0.3	0.4	0.4	0.4	0.5	0.5	0.6	0.6	0.6	0.7	0.7	0.8	0.8	0.8	0.9	0.9	1.0
11	0.3	0.3	0.4	0.4	0.4	0.5	0.5	0.6	0.6	0.6	0.7	0.7	0.7	0.8	0.8	0.8	0.9
10	0.3	0.3	0.3	0.4	0.4	0.4	0.5	0.5	0.5	0.6	0.6	0.6	0.7	0.7	0.7	0.8	0.8
9	0.2	0.3	0.3	0.3	0.4	0.4	0.4	0.5	0.5	0.5	0.5	0.6	0.6	0.6	0.7	0.7	0.7
8	0.2	0.2	0.3	0.3	0.3	0.3	0.4	0.4	0.4	0.5	0.5	0.5	0.5	0.6	0.6	0.6	0.6
7	0.2	0.2	0.2	0.3	0.3	0.3	0.3	0.4	0.4	0.4	0.4	0.4	0.5	0.5	0.5	0.5	0.6
6	0.2	0.2	0.2	0.2	0.2	0.3	0.3	0.3	0.3	0.3	0.4	0.4	0.4	0.4	0.4	0.5	0.5

NOTE: Paint is in gallons, ceiling and wall widths and lengths are in feet.

Tips for Working with Paint

How to Work With and Store Paint

Don't work from your gallon can of paint after it's been opened and stirred. Pour about a quart into a work bucket, and put the lid back on the gallon can while you're working. Only hammer it closed when you're done with the project. Use a finish nail to punch a few holes in the top groove that holds the lip of the lid. This allows paint to drain back into the can, instead of building up in the groove and cause sealing trouble. If you live where the temperature regularly lurks below the freezing mark, don't store latex paint in your garage. Latex paint will freeze. Once it's frozen, the pigments separate and it will lose some of its durability. Always leave a supply of each color of paint to be used for touch ups, even though it may never be used. Clearly mark on each can the room in which the paint was applied and when. Opened paint won't last long—not much more than two years. If interior paint forms a skin, strain it through pantyhose. Unopened paint will last a long time—10 years or more. Store cans away from moisture. Most paint stores won't shake rusty old cans for fear they'll fall apart in the shaker.

Best Way to Clean Latex Paint Rollers

The best way to clean a roller full of latex paint is to leave the sleeve on the roller and place it on end in the roller pan. Using a putty knife, scrape the paint down the side of the roller into the pan.

Turn the roller slightly each time to scrape all sides from top to bottom. After you get rid of as much paint as possible, it will be much easier to wash the remaining paint out of the sleeve. Wash the roller with good bar soap and water (too many forget the soap). Then rinse well in clear water. Store the roller on end so water will drain from it.

Avoid Screens When You Paint

When painting near screens, remove them or slide them out of the way if they're combination windows. If you can't remove porch screens, be careful to cover them with drop cloths. Getting paint out of a screen is difficult. If you do drip paint, get it while it's still wet. Once the paint has dried, it is difficult to remove. Dip a dry paintbrush in a small amount of mineral spirits if it's oil based paint or soapy water if it's latex paint. Then brush the spot on both sides. The paint should come off if it's still wet. If the paint has dried, you can try to remove it using a pin and cleaning out the lattice.

Choose the Right Brush for Your Paint

When using latex paint use a brush made with manmade bristles, such as polyester or nylon. Natural boar bristle brushes swell with water when used in latex paint. Not only will this swelling reduce the life of the brush by splaying the ends, but while you're using it natural bristles become limp. For oil base paint, use a natural bristle brush for the best results. A synthetic brush can be used, but it won't carry as much paint or lay as smoothly as a natural bristle brush.

Using Glues and Adhesives

The surfaces to be glued together must be smooth and free of dirt, grease and old glue. Observe label instructions carefully. Take proper note of temperature and moisture requirements. Sand or plane board edges to be sure they match and fit together. Most glues won't fill gaps. To get a tight-fitting wood joint, buy a hand held planer. Use glue sparingly, more glue is not better. The thinner the glue, the better the bond. All-purpose household glues work well for most of your repair needs. For repairing expensive items such as fine china or furniture, ask your dealer to suggest a glue made specifically for your purpose, or consider having the repair professionally done. Handle all glues and adhesives with care. Use them with plenty of ventilation, and avoid skin or eye contact with the glues. Here is a quick look at glues and adhesives that will do almost any job you have at hand.

Glue/Adhesive	Common Uses	Characteristics/Recommendations
Acrylic	Bonds glass, metal, wood. Indoor and outdoor use.	Very strong bond. Sets in 5 min.; waterproof; dries tan; cures overnight.
Aliphatic (Yellow/Carpenters Glue)	Woodwork/Furniture/Cabinet repair & building.	Clamp for 30 minutes; cures in 12-18 hrs.;water soluble; dries clear.
Contact cement	Bonding laminate plastic to countertops, veneers.	Immediate bonding. Look for waterbased, nonflammable contact cement; dries flexible.
Cyanocrylate (Super/Instant Glue)	Glass, some plastics, rubber, metal, ceramics, and vinyl. Gel for wood.	Weakens in temp. above 150 degrees. Deteriorates when exposed to weather; non-flexible.
Epoxy	Metal, rubber, glass; most materials.	Bonds unlike materials; strong, durable, water resistant; non-flexible; clamp for 2 hrs.
Hot Melt	Leather, fabrics, toys, wood joints, ceramics.	Good for quick fixes. Weaker bond than most adhesives.
Polyvinyl acetate (PVA/White Glue)	Use on porous materials; paper, cloth, pottery, wood.	Clamp for 30 minutes; not water resistant; dries clear; cures in 18-24 hrs.; nonflammable.
Resorcinol	Strong on wood, concrete, leather. Indoor and outdoor.	Cures in 3-10 hrs. depending on temp.; waterproof; dries red; clamps required.
Silicone Adhesives	Metal, glass, fiberglass and wood.	Dries flexible in clear or colors; waterproof; good in all temperatures; clamps not required.

Based on the Member surveys we conduct after each issue, the Tip Trader section is one of the most widely read and popular sections in each issue of our official Club Magazine, American How-To. Here is a place for adding your own tips. We want you to record them as you're working so you'll have them at your fingertips the next time the call goes out for more tips.

Date	Materials	Tip

Date	Materials	Tip

Notes

Notes

Index

Index

Index

Index